KENNY Mac E D1550180 S enior member
of the Shadow Cab. nny is now Deputy
Leader of the Parliamentary Group and has held portfolios covering
enterprise, transport, tourism, telecommunications and justice. He is a
former long standing member of the SNP's NEC and has been National
Treasurer and Vice Convener of Policy. Kenny was also the SNP's Poll Tax
spo' erson, leading the party's popular 'Can Pay, Won't Pay' campaign.
K vas educated at Linlithgow Academy and Edinburgh University, and
senior partner in a law firm until becoming an MSP. He is married
o sons.

s generated from sales of this book will be paid to Scottish
Social and Economic Research.
Press is an independently owned and managed book publishing
based in Scotland, and is not aligned to any political party or

points is an occasional series exploring issues of current and
levance.

Building A Nation

Post Devolution Nationalism in Scotland

KENNY MacASKILL

Luath Press Limited

EDINBURGH

www.luath.co.uk

First Edition 2004
Reprinted 2008

The paper used in this book is acid-free, recyclable and biodegradable.
It is made from low-chlorine pulps produced in a low energy,
low-emission manner from renewable forests.

Printed and bound by
Exacta Print, Glasgow

Typeset in Sabon by
3btype.com 0131 658 1763

Acknowledgements

THIS BOOK COULD NOT have been written without the assistance of many. However, thanks are due in particular to Craig Milroy who was instrumental in its instigation and essential for its completion. His assistance and input along with that of Euan Lloyd and David Hutchison was invaluable. They participated and aided from start to finish. Without them it could not have been achieved. Thanks are also due to Karen Newton and Tricia Marwick who have been supportive and helpful throughout.

Contents

Foreword

THE DISILLUSIONMENT THAT FOLLOWED Devolution was inevitable. An expectations gap existed: what was expected of Devolution and what could be delivered differed markedly. Disillusionment has brought cynicism and disengagement in its wake. Those who were most committed to the cause of Scottish self-government have won the institutions they campaigned so long for, but appear to have lost out in other respects. This has not only affected the SNP though that party has been most obviously affected. Others have been affected too. Scottish Labour's progressive forces have been side-lined. The radicalism of Scottish Labour Action has been swallowed up in the pursuit of power at any price or marginalised to the backbenches where Labour's best talent now sits in the Edinburgh Parliament. The Tories, inveterate opponents of Devolution before its arrival, at times appear to have come to terms with Devolution better than any of the pro-home rule parties and it is their socio-economic agenda that dominates Scottish politics today. Is this what Devolution was supposed to be about?

It has been common in Northern Ireland to refer to a policy deficit as politics there focused hermetically on the constitution. To a lesser extent, that too has been true of Scotland. During the 18 years of Conservative rule that ended in 1997, each of the opposition parties in Scotland focused primarily on two things: opposition to the Tories and Scotland's constitutional status. The Conservatives alone shaped the socio-economic political agenda. The irony of Devolution is that while new self-governing institutions have been won, these are used for a decidedly right-wing agenda. Circumstances conspired against progressive forces but laziness and timidity have played a part.

But if disillusionment was inevitable, that need not mean that it must always prevail. Politics is shaped by contexts beyond the power of any politician or party but not entirely. An old divide is opening up in Scotland between those who, for a variety of reasons, are secure wallowing in disillusionment or are happy with the status quo, and those who are impatient for change and the opportunity to shape Scotland's future. This divide does not conform neatly with either the old left-right or Unionist-Nationalist divides. Small 'c' conservatives are to be found across these political divides.

This book is important in three respects. First, it acknowledges and explains the current disillusionment and does so honestly and self-critically. The SNP is not spared in this analysis. Secondly, the book engages seriously with difficult issues. Some of these issues and problems are common to social democrats everywhere, others are particular to Scotland. At times over the past five years, it seemed that social democrats everywhere except Scotland were grappling with the issues discussed here. Thirdly, there is an underlying and powerful message of optimism, a quiet self-confidence which challenges what Kenny MacAskill calls the 'outward swagger but huge inner self-doubt'. The book may be primarily addressed to a Nationalist audience but should be read well beyond supporters of constitutional independence.

Many years ago, the distinguished American historian Jack Greene noted that 'What independence meant to the members of the Revolutionary generation has received surprisingly little explicit or systematic attention from historians'. Few historians had troubled themselves to look beyond the rhetoric of independence and consider its multi-faceted meanings. Independence had a constitutional-legal meaning but it also had other meanings which were central to those who forged the entity which, only a few years before independence, could not even be called a nation, let alone an entity supporting independence. This book is an important, possibly seminal, contribution to a debate that reflects on the meaning of independence, not just in terms of its constitutional-legal meanings but its wider meanings. It is challenging and provocative in the very best sense.

James Mitchell
September 2004

Introduction

SCOTLAND IS AN ANCIENT NATION. Forged on the anvil of wars of Independence and inveigled into the British State against the wishes of its people. Notwithstanding the loss of its National Parliament and its absorption into a powerful Union, it maintained its distinctive identity for 300 years. Now following the return of that Institution it finds itself at a political crossroads. Does it remain one of the Nations and Regions of the United Kingdom or does it march on to Independence?

Where stands Scotland post Devolution and what is the future for Nationalism in a devolved Parliament? Is the Scottish Parliament a Unionist dead end or a Nationalist Highway to Independence? Has Devolution killed the SNP stone dead or given it a platform to build from? These are questions that need answered as Scotland begins to come to terms with Devolution and decides where to go next.

The years following the re-establishment of the Scottish Parliament have been difficult ones. The defeat of Thatcherism left a legacy of an embattled and embittered land. Eighteen years of Tory rule left a country reeling from huge social and economic changes and yet containing a society with an outward swagger but huge inner self-doubt. Scotland was devoid of self-confidence and uncertain of its direction. Devolution offered the possibility of self-government within the safety of the Union for some, and the stepping-stone to Independence for others.

The vote in favour of a Parliament with tax raising powers was overwhelming. The collective joy on the official opening was there for all to see. Scotland travelled expectantly and euphorically to the Mound even if what was to be done was uncertain and how it was to be achieved was unclear. That Devolution had arrived was all that mattered. Whether it could deliver was not considered. It was to live the Nation's dream not the devolved reality.

Joy and optimism soon faded to be replaced by a corrosive cynicism. Mistakes were made and gaffes were many. But fundamentally an Institution with limited powers could never achieve the ambitions let alone the dreams of an expectant people. The debacle of the Holyrood Building became symptomatic of the ills and failings of Devolution. Hopes and aspirations seemed dashed and a new Scottish Parliament seemed simply to offer more of the same old British failures. Scotland turned both in and on itself. Four years on the Parliament faced a boycott by the electorate. The 2003 Parliamentary elections saw almost as many people abstain from voting as had voted for its creation in the referendum. A warning shot had been fired at the body politic in Scotland.

The SNP as the Party championing self-government and reflecting national self-confidence both gained and suffered most. 1999 saw a Party on the fringes and margins of UK politics become the major Party of opposition in an Institution of some power and focus. As with the Parliament as a whole tensions arose within the Party over purpose and direction. In the 2003 elections it suffered greatest and most publicly. Some of the loss of support was understandable, some self-inflicted. Those who had cherished the hope of a Parliament and supported the cause throughout were most aggrieved by its failings. They turned against it and away from the Party most strongly identified with it. At the same time the Party became riddled with self-doubt and uncertain of its purpose. Was the Parliament a base for or a barrier to Independence? Was it to be worked within or worked against? Factionalism and feuding prevailed and the SNP suffered accordingly.

The opening of the new building offers hope for a fresh start for the Parliament and an opportunity for the SNP to move on. The debate must move on from what was done in the building of Holyrood to what is being done in the Holyrood Building. Expectations will no longer be unrealistically high but achievement will be expected. Self-confidence is beginning to seep into the Scottish people and that should be led by the ambitions of their politicians. Scotland is moving on and will move on from and through its Parliament. This is the only Parliament Scotland has and was one she lost for nigh on 300 years. A devolved Parliament with limited powers is still better than no Parliament and no powers. Criticism from Unionist opponents is to be expected but Nationalists who constantly denigrate it undermine the only base from which Independence will be realised. It might not be the finished article but it is the only Institution that offers the catalyst to Independence.

Scotland is in transition but what to? It's a journey being made not just in the Devolution settlement but also in all aspects of Scottish society. From the constitution to the economy and from religion to race Scotland is changing. Pressured from without by the effects of Globalisation and pushed from within by a Parliament growing in powers and stature. It is a small Nation on the periphery of an enlarged EU and a shrinking world. Post 9/11 and its fall out what is clear is that all Nations no matter how big and powerful are interdependent. What then does Independence mean in an interdependent world and why is it relevant?

The purpose of this book is to show that Independence is essential if the dreams and aspirations of the people of Scotland held at the outset of the establishment of the Parliament and before are to be achieved. That Independence is not inconsistent with an interdependent world but essential to participating in it. The powers of a Nation State may evolve but being one remains the prerequisite to participation in matters dealt with collectively by Nation States.

Likewise the role of the State may change but it remains the engine for social and economic progress and the vehicle to protect a unique culture and distinct identity. Scotland can participate or it can spectate.

Changes are occurring globally as well as locally. Scotland is experiencing the same tensions and pressures as other countries. Free trade and liberal economic policies are changing the economic base of the country and the role of the state within it. 'It's the economy stupid' is accepted by almost all. But if low business taxes are essential for competitiveness, how are public services to be improved and maintained? Demography and the longevity of the human race are putting pressures on social services to be provided within a country with a falling population. What then is the vision for a Social Democratic party within these modern constraints and complexities?

So where does that leave the SNP? There is not simply a new Parliament but new political ground. The debate has moved on irrevocably from being a straight forward left/right divide, public or private ownership and the forces of capital versus the forces of labour. It is about an authoritarian versus libertarian state and liberal versus neo-conservative economics. In a modern society communities seek rights and influence as well as the state. In a global economy where and to what extent are market forces to be allowed to apply? Just as Scotland has to become comfortable with Devolution, Globalisation and a New World Order, so the SNP must adapt to the new terrain.

Independence won't be won by one Party alone but delivered by many with the support of the people. The SNP, though, remains fundamental to achieving that goal. It is in the vanguard of a wider Independence movement encompassing both political parties and broader civic society. It requires being a Party that is inclusive not exclusive – working not just with other political parties but people from all walks of life.

This book will argue that the SNP must take Scotland to

Independence by expanding the powers of the Parliament and increasing the ambition and self-confidence of the people. It will argue that the SNP must define itself as a Social Democratic party but recognise that the arguments have moved on and both adapt to and lead the debate. Declaring itself in support of individuals and communities not simply the State. Recognising that a competitive economy is essential if desired social services are to be delivered. Balancing the need for change and reform with the protection of the poorest and most vulnerable. Supporting an EU of Nation States with a social as well as economic agenda; but being prepared to oppose a Council of Ministers or an unelected Commission with a centralising agenda. Fundamentally, leading mainstream Scotland from a position of power on many social, economic and cultural issues – not being on the margins and speaking solely on the constitution.

Throughout the centuries the Scottish people have dreamed of and aspired to not just Nationhood but a land worthy of its people. It was fought for on the field of Bannockburn and campaigned for in the coalfields of Fife. Not just a free and independent land but a just and prosperous one. Not solely for ethnic Scots but all who want to live here. The Scottish Parliament offers that chance. Post Devolution Nationalism is about Building a Nation.

CHAPTER I

Where Stands Scotland Post Devolution?

'stands Scotland where it did?' *Macbeth*, William Shakespeare

THAT DEVOLUTION HAS DISAPPOINTED is clear. Even the most fervent and passionate supporters of self-government are forced to concede that it has failed to live up to the hopes and expectations of so many. When the Parliament was first opened in 1999, cheering crowds thronged the Royal Mile as the procession marched from the Parliament Square to the Mound. The site of the last Parliament convened in 1707 was marched from, to a temporary home in the General Assembly Buildings on the Mound. The symbolism was there for all to see. A new start was being made for an old Institution. Pride and satisfaction was immense and much of Scotland basked in a warm glow.

It did not take long though for the satisfaction to ebb and the warm glow for members to become a cold shoulder from the populace. The mistakes were many and legion. The awarding of medals to members who had done little and delivered nothing was absurd. Initial debates and arguments were not on the subjects of the day but on the salaries and allowances for members. As Scotland anticipated massive social and economic changes its Parliament concentred on internal matters of relevance and interest to themselves alone, or so it seemed.

Rather than concentrating on a Parliament delivering the social and economic changes that Scots yearned for and Scotland badly needed, the major issue became the site and size of a new and opulent building. Why there had to be a rush to bed down the Parliament is for some to explain or the Fraser Inquiry to decide. After all George Washington had served two terms as President before the USA even considered building Washington DC. They concentrated on building up the new United States of America not constructing the Capitol and Senate. However, the unseemly rush and the folly of a building for politicians as opposed to tangible benefits for the people damaged all. Members were all tarred with the same brush whether they had supported it or not. The Parliament and MSPs became the butt of public disdain and uniform contempt.

There is no doubt that many in Labour, and Donald Dewar in particular, were committed to the establishment of a Scottish Parliament. Their desire to deliver a modicum of self-government was tempered by a fear of lighting the flames of Nationalism. The schizophrenia within Labour ranks was shown from the outset. How were they to celebrate the re-establishment of the Nation's Parliament after 300 years and on the back of a landslide vote in its favour? Yet, at the same time, how were they to downplay Nationalist sentiment in a unitary British State? Was it to be a time of national celebration or was it to be downplayed to diminish aspirations and expectations? The official opening accordingly saw a Royal visit but no public holiday and a Concorde fly past but school kids sitting at their desks. That schizophrenia continued. Being an Executive but not a Government. Having the trappings of office but not the power. Labour's choice of site for the new Parliament building was aimed at avoiding a nationalist shibboleth being established on Calton Hill at all costs, a decision that would come back to haunt all.

As a result a Parliament was created with inadequate powers and neutered from the outset. A Federal system at least has logic and symmetry. What was established in Scotland had neither. Powers were reserved or devolved on the grounds of political expediency not good governance. Accordingly absurdities were created such as the Parliament being responsible for justice but not drugs or firearms, roads but not railways and doctors but not vets. More importantly it had none of the fiscal levers necessary for significant social and economic change apart from the ability to vary income tax up or down by up to 3p. A measure of very limited benefit and in any event inadequate to address the problems faced. That meant that the Parliament was incapable of making the substantial economic and policy changes that were desired. Accordingly, in the absence of economic powers it concentrated on a limited social agenda.

The absence of adequate powers resulted in a Parliament seeking to create its mark, not by delivering change, but discussing issues. Yet the people of Scotland wanted action not rhetoric. They had expected significant change and they got little of comfort let alone relevance. Much of the blame can be laid at the door of an Executive that was inept, devoid of vision and uncertain whether it was a Government or a glorified Council. The Institution ended up looking like a debating chamber rather than a legislative Parliament. Faults and gaffes were numerous. Mistakes were many. Some were self-inflicted and others imposed. Some criticism was just and fair, some was misinterpretation or downright distortion of fact. There is, though, neither comfort nor solace in making excuses or apportioning blame.

It was not meant to be thus but arguably it could only ever have been so. Irrespective of mistakes, individual or collective and whether by the Institution or the Executive, compounding matters aspirations could never be reached and delivery never achieved. Hopes were too high and powers too few. The first Parliament in nearly 300 years followed the dark days of Thatcherism. Scotland saw and expected not just light at the end of the tunnel but constant sunshine from the outset. No Parliament could deliver that, and certainly not one lacking adequate fiscal powers never mind responsibility over key areas of social policy whether pensions or benefits.

The Scottish feelings of failure and let down are not unique. There is historical and international precedent. New Parliaments the world over, irrespective of the anvil on which they have been forged, have struggled to sustain and maintain public expectations. From the Irish Free State formed after the Anglo-Irish War, through the Baltic Sates and their secession from the Soviet Union, to Nations such as Poland liberated from the Russian orbit, all have been greeted with huge public acclaim on their creation or emancipation. Yet, they appeared to dash that hope and expectation.

The Irish Free State saw many who had fought in a violent struggle reject what they had achieved as inadequate and not what they had made the ultimate sacrifice for. Poverty and unemployment remained. Emigration continued to plague the Free State Government as it had scarred the British Province. This was not what it was supposed to be like. Freedom was a just and noble cause and yet appeared to bring much of the problems and blights borne in servitude.

Similar situations occurred in the Post Soviet Nations. In Lithuania a people who had faced years of oppression elected President Landsbergis as its founding father. A few years on the man who had faced down Russian tanks and kept the candle of Nationhood alive during the dark years was ejected and replaced by apparatchiks who had collaborated in the old regime. Independence and freedom was not supposed to be about continuing poverty or struggle. Hindsight and nostalgia for old certainties seemed better than the new void. Poland too saw a flourishing of national spirit with the removal of Russian tanks and a puppet regime. Again hopes were high for prosperity and improvement. When this did not immediately occur feelings of depression and disappointment set in.

Scotland is not alone in seeing a new and longed for Institution fail to deliver the immediate changes that have been the subject of dreams and sustained the cause over centuries. The real world is unfortunately different from the dream. Ordinary life is not like a rebel song or a nationalist ballad. Singing about the Merry Plough Boy is vastly different from creating the happy farmer. Real life cannot match the dream. It was the same in Scotland as elsewhere. That is not to excuse the mistakes or forgive the failures. Even if the aspirations could never have been achieved what transpired should have been better. Culpability still remains.

Change, though, can be effected. The quality of life and the state of the economy can be improved. After the initial high followed by a consequent depression realisation sets in that allows for progress and tangible improvements to be achieved. In Ireland it took a generation or more for that change to occur. In Lithuania and in Poland it has already happened and took only a few years. No-one in those lands would seek to forsake their new found Independence or freedom of action. The realisation that change and improvement have to be worked for and that progress takes time allows for a vision of Building a Nation to be created. Scotland too has that opportunity with a new start in the new building.

What is also clear is that Devolution is irrevocable. Notwithstanding the ills and faults of Devolution it has happened and will not be reversed. This is a constitutional highway down which Scotland has set off. The final destination has not been resolved but there is no way back. Devolution is irrevocable even if Independence is not certain.

There is a growing consensus across parties and people that the current devolved settlement is not working. Even those who opposed it at the outset see the solution in making it work effectively not ending it. The status quo is not an option and the Parliament needs to move on. That means an improved performance by members, and in particular the Executive, but it also means greater powers. Limited additional powers have been ceded but more and in particular enhanced fiscal powers are required. If the Institution is to deliver it needs the means and mechanisms to do so. Devolution after all is a process not an event.

The Constitutional debate is ongoing and the argument is about what further powers should be devolved and how far and fast the process should proceed. There are a few individual and siren voices calling for a return to direct rule from Westminster. They are without power and influence and remain firmly on the margins. Whether failed Tory candidates or defeated Tory Lords their day has passed and their influence has ebbed. Overwhelmingly, those who opposed Devolution at the outset now accept its arrival. The evidence of that is clear from the actions and attitudes of the Scottish Conservative Party. Wiped out in the final overthrow of Thatcherism they opposed the breaking up of the Union and the creation of a Devolved Administration. The Parliament though offered a lifeline which they have not only grasped but arguably grappled with successfully. The Conservatives now accept Devolution as a matter of fact and foreswear any repudiation or cessation of it. Whilst publicly refusing to argue for further Devolution or transfer of powers they have neither rejected enhanced powers that have been further devolved nor reined in prominent members calling for more. Whilst many of them argue for Fiscal Autonomy from a neo-conservative ideological stance as opposed to a Scottish constitutional position the outcome is still the same.

So, Scotland stands with a Parliament that has disappointed but will be given a further opportunity to deliver. What has occurred is regrettable and some is unforgivable. But, Scotland cannot stand still and must move on. As with other Nations it must pick itself up from initial disappointment. Scotland is receiving a second chance on the back of the opening of the new building. That chance must be taken and cannot be spurned. The Parliament needs to be relevant and be able to react to the wants and needs of the people. To be able to live up to even limited aspirations, never mind the dreams of the Scottish people, the Parliament needs to increase its powers. What powers are then required, and how do you Build an Independent Nation in an Interdependent world?

CHAPTER 2

Independence, Interdependence or both?

'to be free is to have access to a myriad of interdependent relationships with others.'

Jeremy Rifkin

AT THE SAME TIME as the argument on Independence has been ongoing it has become clearer that all Nations are Interdependent. It's
not simply a shrinking world in terms of international travel or a
growing uniformity of culture and media. The development of a
global economy has restricted the freedom of action of every land.
The role of Government as well as its powers has been transformed.
Many services and industries are no longer owned let alone operated
by the State. Nor are they even run by a national company but an
international corporation. Is Independence therefore an historical
anachronism or does it remain a necessity in the modern world?
Does the Nation State have any relevance any more or is it an outdated Nationalist concept?

But why is it an either/or argument? Why are the two positions
viewed as being mutually exclusive? Surely, the position is that Nation
States are all Independent but also Interdependent. That position
applies to a greater or lesser extent to all Nations even the most
powerful ones. Post 9/11 and the Iraq conflict it is clear that even
the most powerful Nation the world has ever known, the USA, cannot
insulate itself from world events nor isolate itself from the international community.

Similarly, as the global economy and international trade develop
countries are all mutually entwined. The price of oil is affected not

just by world events but by there being a world economy. It's not simply conflict in Iraq or tension in the Gulf that sends the price of a barrel of oil soaring, but competition for a finite resource whether from China or South East Asia. Similarly, the health of the American economy, due to its size and influence, affects the well being of all others whether they like it or not. In a global economy sickness is contagious, and when America sneezes the world catches cold.

Nations are becoming ever more Interdependent, and not just in an enlarged EU with or without a formal constitution. What is clear and will remain so is that the constituent part of the interdependency is the Nation State. It is the building block upon which interdependency and international co-operation are founded. If you are not a Nation State then you are not represented. It matters not whether you are an economically powerful region like Bavaria or California nor an ancient nation such as Scotland or Catalonia. Whether in the United Nations or the EU the representatives come not from Regions but Nation States. Regions no matter how big or powerful are excluded. Nations no matter how small or poor are included. Hence Micronesian atolls have representation in the UN but Scotland does not. Luxembourg could vote in the EU on the destruction of the Scottish fishing fleet, Scotland could not.

Interdependency will grow as the global economy extends and the EU expands but Statehood will remain the key to representation. That is clear within the EU as elsewhere. Regions may be recognised and committees formed to reflect them. They remain, though, subordinate in powers and influence and always will. It's the Nation States that vote and just as importantly possess a veto. Luxembourg and Malta can. Scotland and Catalonia cannot. A devolved Scotland even with many enhanced powers is not and never will sit at the top table. That is why Independence remains essential. It is not simply the symbolism of an ancient Nation once again being formally recognised. It is the power to defend our existing industries and grow new ones.

It's the same for international relations as it is in the economic sphere. Notwithstanding the unilateral action by the UK and the USA in the Iraq conflict, international co-operation will grow and develop. It becomes clearer by the day and by the death that the only way to extricate the Atlantic axis from Iraq is to internationalise the situation. Whilst Scots could march in their hundreds of thousands and the Scottish Parliament could debate the rights and wrongs of the conflict, orders were issued from elsewhere. The orders for the troops were dispatched from London and the international debates saw Scotland excluded not just from the Security Council but the UN chamber. If you wish to take responsibility for whether you wage war and whether your young men go off to a conflict in a foreign field you need relevant powers. If you wish to say that it is not in your name then you need to be able to be heard in the Institutions that matter.

That said, in the New World, more and more matters will be dealt with on a transnational and intergovernmental basis. In most instances that is no bad thing. Whether it's as a result of the internationalising of the world economy or the addressing of health or environmental crises, collective action is both welcome and necessary. The environment and many other areas recognise no national boundaries and co-operation is essential. Chernobyl and the SARS epidemic are testament to that. Even in terms of opposing many of the problems of Globalisation, of which there are many, the only solution is to act on a co-operative basis to achieve the required strength and united action.

The Nation State though has changed in a multitude of ways. It's not simply co-operation at EU or international level. One Crown, One Faith, One Flag was always a myth but many of the totems of Nationhood no longer exist. Uniform passports within the EU, along with a common currency within the Euro zone have dispensed with what were once symbols of the State. The Schengen agreement sees the abandonment of border posts between many lands within the EU.

Co-operation and sharing is becoming the norm whether in military or economic spheres. That is an opportunity for Scotland rather than a dilution of the identity to be achieved.

When the Irish Free State was formed, postboxes were painted a different colour and the motif changed to show the passing of the Crown and the establishment of a new order. Similar changes occurred in a myriad of other spheres. Such changes now are neither necessary to create a modern Nation, nor applicable where EU and other directives are opening up postal deliveries and a range of other public services to international not just private competition. The whole role of the State is being transformed in terms of what it provides and what it does not. The existence of a Nation State is no longer dictated by leitmotifs on a variety of services or a different name or colour for some organisations. It is defined by representation in the Institutions that matter and control over functions that are essential to the economy and a distinctive society.

As well as being unable to avoid the changes to the Nation State that have arisen internationally, Scotland cannot ignore its geography. It is situated on a small island with its major trading partner adjacent to it. British economies and societies are intertwined in a myriad of ways. Independent representation in the international arena does not mean isolation and dislocation within the Island of Britain. Scandinavian Nations have cross-border arrangements and transnational co-operation that preceded the establishment of the EEC and exceeds what is dictated by the EU. They recognise and build on their unique geography, shared history and common interests but do so as Independent States. That can and should be replicated here.

Similarly on the Island of Britain actions need to be taken that allow both the independent representation of the separate Nations and co-operation between them. Given the nature of modern economies and the interlinking of societies some matters will require to be dealt with on an intra island basis. Two Nations One Island. Wales is also on a Nation on the mainland of Britain but it has no land border with Scotland. It will be for the people of Wales to decide the pace and extent of their constitutional journey. The concept of Two Nations One Island is already being practised across the Irish Sea. Two Irelands One Island. That means shared authorities not London dictat. Direct representation of interests and the right to both vote and veto on cross-border authorities, not simply to accept what London perceives as good for Scotland. Areas such as transport, telecommunications and energy are prime examples. Cross-border trains require a cross-border authority. Not one directed from London but representing common interests. In telecommunications, how other than by a shared authority can mobile phones or other matters in the Border areas be regulated? Similarly in energy if gas is being imported from east of the Urals or from across the North Sea by a multinational company there is no need for totems of national identity to run it, but a clear need for representation at supra national level to regulate it.

Global changes never mind British geography and a shared history over three hundred years lead to a different solution for Scotland than other Nations becoming independent in the past. The political United Kingdom will wither but the physical island of Great Britain will remain. Scotland can liberate itself politically but not geographically. That means a distinct solution, especially when it is accepted that the days of repainting the postboxes or adding a different motif are past. That means a distinct solution modelled in part on the likes of Scandinavia but accepting the uniqueness of the Scottish position. A recognition that some matters need addressed at supra national level, others on an intra island basis but at all times remembering that power is retained by the sovereign Scottish Parliament and only ceded by it on merit.

Is there a need for a separate DVLA or even Ordnance Survey? If you can differentiate between petrol engines and diesel engines why not between excise duty north and south of the Border? Instructions and directions can be given and costs shared. Does a bureaucracy need to be created in Saltcoats as well as in Swansea? Do we need a separate Department of War Graves? Can we not simply pay our share as well as our respects? Do we need to reinvent the Civil Aviation Authority or other such Institutions as opposed to exercising control from north of the border even if the Institution remains located south of it. Can we not ensure that directions and instructions are given and our interest achieved without an additional bureaucracy? There are numerous other organisations and Departments where separation is not necessary but the right to direct and instruct is.

That is not the abandonment of Nationhood. It is an acceptance of the more complex world in which we live. It constitutes an understanding of the shared history that we have and the small island on which we are located and a recognition that Nationhood is about power and influence more than administration and bureaucracy. In any event many of these matters are being harmonised and will be dealt with on a European not simply a UK basis.

Scotland with full fiscal powers and with independent representation in the EU and UN will need to concentre on wealth creation not a burgeoning civil service. Independence will be achieved and best served by the strength of our economy not the size of our bureaucracy. Better jobs that grow the economy rather than shuffle paper in a hard and competitive world. If real power is obtained and if control can be exercised, the location of the administrators whether Edinburgh, London or Brussels becomes irrelevant. Independence in the twenty first century is about political and fiscal control even if that means through some shared Institutions or common services whether within the British Islands or the EU.

Where stands Scotland in that context? Independence remains absolutely essential; not simply for cultural sympathy or historic sentiment. Without it Scotland can neither participate at nor be heard in the forums or organisations that matter. Holyrood can huff and puff but the winds of change blow from elsewhere. Independence has moved on from the Braveheart era if that was ever really the case in any event. But some things remain constant, such as Independent representation within the EU and the United Nations; Fiscal Autonomy to decide who to tax, what to tax, the rate to tax it at and what to spend it on. They remain fundamental. Many other matters will require to be dealt with in a partnership based on the equality of Nation States. That is something that operates perfectly normally and harmoniously elsewhere in Europe. In Scandinavia some matters are dealt with at EU level, others at a Scandic level but at all times key decisions ranging from what they tax and what they spend it on to whether to live at war or in peace are made by the Nation State. Scotland on the Island of Britain and in the EU should be no different.

Independence and Interdependence are not mutually irreconcilable but absolutely essential. Co-operation is beneficial and necessary. However, full fiscal freedom and independent representation in the EU and UN are fundamental. Independence is the foundation on which a Nation can be built.

CHAPTER 3

The Scottish Parliament – a base for or a barrier to Independence?

'It gives us freedom, not the ultimate freedom that all nations desire and develop to, but the freedom to achieve it'

Michael Collins, 19 December 1921

THE SNP, MORE THAN other political parties, had difficulties in adjusting to Devolution. That's perhaps unsurprising given both its commitment to Independence and its history with previous Devolution campaigns. It is a debate that has been ongoing in the Nationalist movement since its very inception and throughout the campaign for a Parliament. Does it advance Scotland or does it not? Is it a base for a further push to Independence or a barrier to its ever being achieved? It has ravaged the SNP and formed schisms and dividing lines more so than on the traditional left-right spectrum. These debates were both fundamental and legitimate in the days before the Parliament was constituted. They must, though, be resolved if the Party is to go forward within the new Institution.

In any event they are no longer relevant with the arrival of the Parliament, and the fact that it's here to stay. This is the only Parliament the Scots have of their own and it's up to them to make of it what they will. It can remain as a devolved Institution within the British State, or it can move on to sovereign status. What it cannot be is torn down and built anew. Do that and its not another 300 years that Scotland will wait, but forever. Moreover, it is the only Institution that offers both the base and catalyst to achieve Nationhood. Independence will come through the Parliament or not at all.

The divide within the SNP is historically unsurprising. The party was formed in the wave of Nationalism that swept over the land with the National Covenant resulting in the union of an explicit Independence party with a home rule party equivocal on Independence. Throughout its short history it has listened to other Parties whether in power or opposition talk of their concern for Scotland and the need for a Scottish Parliament. At the same time the Scots continued to suffer and Scotland continued to lose out. Factories closed and industries declined. Emigration bled the country of many of the young and the most talented. Corporate takeovers and cultural assimilation continued unabated. From Maxton and the ILP through to Ted Heath and the Tories' Declaration of Perth, pledges were made and promises were broken. Innumerable Labour politicians came and went and still Keir Hardie's vision remained a mirage. Nationalists were right to be sceptical of Unionists' promises.

The political rise of the SNP in the 1970s saw the debate continue both in the Party and in the country. The Nationalist threat saw a Devolved Assembly offered. What was the Party of Independence to do? Would it support it or reject it? After much soul searching the Party agreed to back it. After all, then as now, it offered something tangible even if inadequate. However, the machinations and chicanery of the Labour Government left the SNP scarred and Scotland the loser. The powers of the proposed Assembly where whittled down and schemed against. Before their very eyes Nationalists who had been sceptical but prepared to unite for the common cause saw it evaporate. Their efforts were not matched by consequent support from within Labour ranks. Instead, they were met in many instances by opposition from within that Party not only to the Assembly but its own Government's fortunes.

Despite the lacklustre support by the Labour Government and the absence of support from many Labour activists a majority, albeit a small one, was delivered for devolution in 1979. However, as a result of an outrageously anti-democratic 40 per cent rule instigated by George Cunningham, a Labour backbench MP, Devolution was lost. Emotionally understandably, if not politically astutely, the SNP representatives in Westminster voted with the Opposition to bring down Jim Callaghan's Government. That vote had been mandated on them by SNP members who burned with rage at what had been done to the dream of even a modicum of self-government. The SNP was accused of having brought down the Labour Government and un-leashing Thatcherism upon Scotland. The truth was that Callaghan's administration had been brought down by its own economic ineptitude rather than the consequences of its constitutional failures. The failings of the Labour Government and faults within the Labour Party delayed the Parliament for another twenty years. Perception, however, is as important as reality. The Tartan Tory myth was created and both Scotland and the SNP turned in on themselves.

The outcome of the referendum was damaging to both Scotland and the SNP. The SNP paid a heavy political penalty and Scotland paid a high social and economic price. Those Labour opponents of Devolution left Scotland unprotected and powerless to 18 years of Tory rule from London. The myth of a united British working class left a Scottish working class devastated in its wake. As much of blue collar England went Tory most of Scotland paid the price. The damage was not just to the economy but to the National psyche. If an Assembly with only modest powers couldn't be won what ever could be? Scottish self-confidence was further shattered and ebbed away. SNP faith in doing deals on Devolution and co-operating for constitutional powers was sapped.

The aspiration for a Parliament and the dream of Independence continued albeit weakened and diminished. Labour grew stronger than ever in Scotland. But its rhetoric about making the land un-governable was met by Tory legislation in Westminster imposing the Poll Tax. SNP scepticism with Labour promises remained. That continued on and through the creation of a Constitutional Convention.

This was after all a vehicle that the SNP had initially championed and supported, but on its birth veered away from. The Party had campaigned for a convention as a way of separating the constitution from other political factors, in order to allow people to vote on their preferred constitutional relationship not simply on the handling of the economy or the ousting of a hated Tory Govern-ment. The exclusion of Independence from possible constitutional outcomes saw it boycott the proceedings. Rather than a route to improve Scotland's political position it was perceived as a barrier to the Party's ultimate goal.

Fears of Independence being excluded and even diluted powers being sold out again resulted in the Party's abstention. Similar thoughts arose with the return of a New Labour Government and its commitment to a Scottish Parliament? Was New Labour genuine, and if they were, why were they doing it? It must be a devolutionary trap or so many thought. After inner soul searching and much reflection the Party agreed to support the proposals for a Scottish Parliament and campaign for a Yes/Yes vote. A decision that was necessary not only to achieve the required result, but also to avoid leaving an electorate bemused that Scotland's Party would oppose a Scottish Parliament. Refusing to support a devolved Parliament would have baffled an electorate that would assume that the SNP would support any Parliament as opposed to no Parliament. It would have appeared that constitutional technicalities and political sectarianism were being placed before the National interest. That would have been a political disaster for Scotland's Party. Thankfully that did not occur. The Party supported the campaign for a Yes/Yes vote. A united front in Scotland opposed only by a rump of discredited Tories saw a landslide victory. People voted, overwhelmingly, not just for their own Parliament once again but also for one able to raise its own taxes.

A pre-legislative referendum had seen many Scots vote in the expectation that it would be a Parliament with powers and teeth. However, as detailed earlier, powers were reserved or withheld in a variety of areas leaving an emasculated Parliament. In many instances those granted fell far short of what had been anticipated, even though it had been accepted from the outset that it would not be a fully independent authority. That too left a sour taste in the mouths of many nationalists. Areas of responsibility that it had assumed would be devolved were not and the Parliament was the weaker for it. So that is how the SNP's view of the Parliament was forged and formed.

The SNP is not unique in this internal debate. It has afflicted and affected almost every other nationalist movement throughout history. Do you try to proceed gradually and incrementally gaining footholds here and there and building up credibility and confidence? Or do you hold out for the true ideal, refusing to either compromise or to be compromised? There are arguments for and against both routes and methods. Asking for half a loaf might see you offered nothing but holding out for the whole loaf might see you starve. It even resulted in a civil war in Ireland and brought about the death of one of that Nation's founding fathers in Michael Collins.

Whilst there is historical precedent along with recent reasoning why the Party is sceptical of the Parliament and unsure of its role, that must be resolved if both the Parliament and the Party are to go forward. There requires to be a clear demarcation between the actions of the Executive and the role of the Parliament. Much of the difficulty faced by the SNP has been caused by the failure of the public to distinguish between the two. The incompetence of the Executive is visited upon all the members of the Parliament. The ills of the Lib/Lab administration were visited upon the SNP as much as the incumbent administration. That will change. It will resolve itself as greater scrutiny is applied and a new view is taken of the Institution.

There are two key reasons why the SNP must now support not disparage the Parliament. It must recognise that its role is to build up the Institution and take power within it. The first is that it is the only realistic route by which Independence can be obtained. Take power within it or forever be powerless to deliver Independence. The second is it that it is the only Parliament that Scotland has, even if its powers are inadequate. Confidence and faith in it will be symptomatic of belief and self-esteem outwith it. Scotland's politicians, especially Nationalists, must have confidence in the Institution for the public to be asked to trust it. For, if the Scots don't have some faith in their Parliament they won't have belief in themselves, or their Nation, never mind Independence.

Every Nation is unique but it is possible to look for historical precedents and examples. That applies in how Nations achieve Independence and self-government as much as it does in other spheres. What is clear is that the most common reasons for the creation of a newly independent Nation will not apply here. That is that they arose following economic collapse, the end of a dynasty or dislocation brought about by war. That is neither likely to happen, nor wanted by anyone. There is no desire for revolution or armed insurrection and the SNP has quite properly and correctly denounced any such attempts. Even the end of the House of Windsor would not compare with the collapse of the Romanovs or the end of the Austro-Hungarian Empire.

Scotland will move forward from within rather from without. Whilst the catalyst for and the speed of movement will be dictated by events from outwith, it will be for the Parliament to seek more powers and be granted the authority and legitimacy needed through a referendum. To do that requires taking powers within the Devolved Administration. A similar pattern of events occurred in some of the most recent Nations States formed in Europe. The Baltic States succeeded by using the base of their Federated Parliaments to organise and win referenda. Without the legitimacy, never mind the bureaucracy, contained within those Institutions, then secession from the Soviet Union would have been difficult if not impossible.

It's not just historically how Scotland is likely to become an Independent Nation but democratically the proper way. Some still argue for the 'big bang' theory of Nationalism. That sufficient shouting of Independence will see the Scots replicate Paul on the Road to Damascus and set off with renewed faith to vote for Independence in an election. That all that is required is the return to the faith and the election will provide the mandate for the Party of Independence. If only it were as simple as that! But, it's not just how but in which election? How can you win in a Westminster Parliament dominated by English votes? How could a majority of Nationalist MPs deliver Independence against a Holyrood administration not supportive of it? The return of a majority in Holyrood can only be a mandate for a referendum.

People vote on a multitude of factors – social and economic as well as constitutional. Support for a Party is usually given on a broad range of matters not simply one specific cause. An administration can be both won and formed on a minority of votes. To seek to impose a major constitutional change in these circumstances would be wrong. It would also be unsuccessful. Scotland can only succeed in Independence if it is what the majority of the people want. The criticism of the Referendum strategy is that people are encouraged to vote for the SNP even if they are sceptical about Independence. But why is that a bad thing? Surely the SNP should seek and accept votes from as wide a range of people as possible. If they are prepared to put their trust in an SNP Administration surely it is better to accept their votes than reject them. To show that you are competent and fit to Govern but that your abilities and those of the Nation are constrained by the lack of powers. Accepting their votes conditionally allows an opportunity to prove yourself and build up the confidence of those who are doubters. Better that than rejecting them out of hand. In any event it's what is done by the Party at local authority level and has proved highly successful in many areas. An 'ideologically pure' Party may appeal to some but not the electorate. Independence can only come about when it is sought and voted for specifically by a majority of the people. A Scotland that sought to become independent by foisting the decision of a few upon the many would be devoid of legitimacy. The way forward is to form an administration and win a referendum. There is no other way.

Similarly, the formation of a Nationalist administration and the winning of a referendum are contingent upon a confident and forward looking society. A clear component of that society will be a Parliament and people with self-belief and who seek to improve themselves and need the requisite powers to do so. The idea that the SNP gains from Scotland's suffering is not only absurd but wrong. A decline in Scottish self-confidence is matched and mirrored by a decline in the SNP vote. The 1980s was testimony to that. A people who are devoid of faith in themselves are unlikely to aspire to self-determination. The economic suffering of the black population in the USA has seen not a call for greater emancipation but a society that has turned in on itself and in many instances has socially imploded.

A constant denigration of the Parliament is to be expected from its opponents but is unwelcome from its supporters. It's not only unhelpful but positively damaging. That is not to say that where mistakes have been made and errors have occurred that they should not be called to account. However, calling it a 'toy town parliament' denigrates the Institution. The scattergun sniping from the sidelines in many instances shoots the wrong target. It guns down the Parliament not the Executive and injures Scottish self-confidence rather than the British State. A rubbishing of the Institution reflects on all our society. It becomes symptomatic not just of Scots woes but Scots inadequacies. It becomes a self-fulfilling prophecy.

The SNP is committed not just to the achievement of Independence but the creation of a better Scotland. The two are intertwined as stated earlier. A scorched earth policy neither wins hearts and minds nor delivers a land worth having. It is therefore the duty of all who support Independence to seek to make this a better land not just when Independence is achieved but until it is delivered. This is our own, our native land and we should respect and cherish it. These are our people and we are morally obliged to allow them to reach their full potential irrespective of the constitutional settlement that prevails upon them. Besides, to move on to an Independent Parliament Scots need to have faith in their devolved Parliament. That means offering solutions for this life not simply the life hereafter. The SNP needs to be able to address current problems as well as offer a constitutional solution.

The current Parliament might not be the one that we seek but it is the only one that we have. We need to go forward to the one we want from the base of the one that exists. Continued denigration of it simply fans the flames of the fire that burns away at the self-confidence of the Scots. Independence will come not when a minority have the vocal chords to demand it but when the majority have the self-confidence to seek it. That self-confidence is growing and will be determined by social, economic and cultural factors not just constitutional ones. A generation is growing up who have no concept of a Scotland without a Parliament, as are an electorate who now view it as part of the political landscape. Positioning yourself with its opponents as opposed to arguing for its improvement is damaging. The SNP must therefore point out that the inadequacies come about from the Executive's ineffectiveness and the Parliament's powerlessness, not from the Institution itself.

Scotland can be a better place under Devolution but to be the best it can be it must be independent. Taking power within the Parliament is therefore essential for both Independence and the SNP. As Michael Collins said about the Irish Free State 'it gives us freedom, not the ultimate freedom that all nations desire and develop to, but the freedom to achieve it.' That though means being credible as a Party as well as an Institution. The SNP must change its perception if not its outlook. Part of that must be by championing the Parliament as it can be rather than castigating it for being so. It is not a barrier to Independence but the base from which to achieve it. This is the Nation's Parliament. We must build it up to Build the Nation.

CHAPTER 4

A Social Democratic Party or an Independence Pressure Group?

'Politics is divided into those who seek to change the world to suit their ideas and those who seek to modify their actions to suit the world'

Albert Sorel

AS WELL AS A VISION there must be a defined political philosophy that is both credible and understandable. Post Devolution the SNP must outline a coherent manifesto for a Devolved Administration as well as a clear vision for an Independent Nation. That means having a political philosophy capable of being implemented in both, even if constrained in one. It must show not only that it is credible but that what it offers is desirable. People will aspire to Independence only if it is an improvement on what exists and if they have faith in the abilities and talents of those who champion it.

That means outlining and defining Scottish Social Democracy not simply espousing it. It sounds good but what is meant by it? What does it mean for jobs and services never mind the economy and society? It entails outlining what you stand for not simply opposing what the Executive or Opposition are doing. The electorate knows that the SNP stands for Independence. What it is unsure of and in many instances unaware of is what else it stands for. A Party that aspires to Government needs also to be prepared to make the hard choices that go with it. It is important to be clear what the Party stands against. Supporting everything and opposing nothing is equally unpalatable.

The need is not to shout Independence louder but outline the social, economic, cultural and environmental case better. Awaiting a political Buggins' turn is not an option. There is a neither a scientific nor political rule that oppositions must become Governments. Hearts need won and minds need persuaded. The Party must outline its vision of a Social Democratic Scotland and look and act like a Government in waiting. It must build up the trust of the people of Scotland and their faith not just in the Party but also in themselves.

Since its very formation there has been an ongoing debate about the purpose and function of the SNP. All agreed that the goal was Independence but how? Was it to be a Party or a Movement? Should it be a broad based pressure group or more focused political Party? Was it to represent all political views or one alone? What was its vision beyond that of an Independent Scotland?

Over the years the SNP realised that being a formal political Party meant taking a fixed position on the political spectrum. To that there was no alternative. In its absence all that exists is a shifting alliance united on Independence but not on other issues. That is a political home built on sand. That coalition can work for a pressure group or allow political parties to co-operate in referenda. It does not work for a political party campaigning in elections or for elected representatives in political office. There a coherent political position is required.

The SNP had difficulties early on in adapting to new found success at local authority level. Elected representatives with differing views on a variety of issues split on the line or vote to take. The Party was perceived as being all things to all men and a different organisation in the rural areas from the central belt. It brought the Party into disrepute and many gains were lost. Similar difficulties have afflicted Independent Councils and other coalitions in Scotland throughout the years.

As a result the SNP adopted a left of centre stance. To be anything other would have been irreconcilable with being Scotland's Party. It was based not simply on the feelings of the Country but represented the views of the membership. Supporters, let alone members of the Party, expect it to stand up for the People not just the Nation. They expect the Party to represent the interests of the community as well as the corporates. On issues from the poll tax to nuclear dumping the SNP, therefore, has and does lead across Scotland for its citizens.

Some argued that it is a mistake to be so defined. That doing so limited the creation of the broadest possible coalition for Independence. But a definition there must be or past mistakes will simply be repeated. Others have argued that the best opportunity is to be located in the centre or on the right. That belies the nature of the Party and the myth, if not the reality, of political culture in Scotland. To describe Scotland as a left-wing country is overly simplistic and denies much of the reality. After all Labour have never had a majority of votes and their vote has been declining. In any event support for them was not necessarily for a left-wing ideology. The perspective is more cultural than political. It is values more than doctrine that define Scottish society. Scotland, however, is most certainly an egalitarian country. It has been forged on an anvil of historical events that have created a culture of equality and of public service. From the days of the Reformation and the creation of parish schools there has been a drive to educate all and for all to participate.

Whether in the urbanised central belt or the rural crofting counties, communities grew up seeing the need for co-operation, whether against the excesses of the landlord or the industrialist. More recently a post war generation benefited from the public services provided, be they municipal housing, comprehensive education or a National Health Service. Many feel a debt of gratitude to a community that provided for them, helped to shape them and allowed them to improve themselves. Finally, the consequences of Thatcherism burned deep into the Scottish soul. The suggestion that there was no such thing as society was a heresy to a Nation with a collective past. The Tories suffered greatly and will wait long for absolution.

The Party defines itself as 'left of centre'. Most accept it and many champion it. But what is meant by this in the changing political climate? The time has come for the Party to flesh out what it means by that and to define itself as Social Democratic in the North European tradition. The term Social Democrat was brought into the UK political lexicon and indeed disrepute by David Owen's short lived but not lamented SDP. However, in broader political terms the Social Democratic label is applied to many parties in Northern Europe and the Scandic countries in particular.

Such Parties have seen the need for private enterprise supported by public provision allowing for a free market in some areas but not all, while accepting that the State has duties and citizens have rights. Fundamentally, Social Democrats believe that it's not just the interests of the consumer that matter but that there is such a thing as society. They have delivered a vibrant economy, a just society and a democratic community. They have balanced the need for a competitive economy with the moral obligation of a fair society. They have opposed injustice and intolerance not just at home but abroad. Many in Scotland look quite rightly with envy at what has been created in Nations like Sweden and Finland, mostly built without the benefit of North Sea oil. In Building a Nation few better examples can be found, and the architects of them were principally Social Democrats. It is that model that the SNP should follow.

If a defined position was necessary before the establishment of the Scottish Parliament then it is even more so now. Parliament means addressing a gamut of issues not all of which have a constitutional basis. Suggesting that all issues have an Independence perspective is absurd. What is the Independence aspect to whether or not prostitution tolerance zones are to be created in our communities? Where lies the constitutional aspect to the debate on congestion charging? What is the sovereignty issue in the boundaries or existence of National Parks? Some issues are related to society, the economy and the environment and apply as much in a devolved Scotland as they would in an Independent one.

A logical and coherent philosophy is therefore needed to address the new political landscape. Being able to do so allows support to be built and power to be obtained in the Parliament. That does not mean that the philosophy is inflexible. Beliefs and ideologies must adapt to changing times and circumstances. Countries' structures and societies vary. Scotland is distinct and will require its own unique solution. In any event even in Sweden and Norway there is recognition by their Social Democratic parties that the global economy and the ageing of the population amongst other factors mean that change is inevitable. However, they are at least a tangible model to follow with societies that mirror Scotland in many ways from the size of their urban centres to a substantial rural hinterland. If Scotland replicates them then she will certainly be healthier, wealthier and wiser. Changes and adaptions to meet the needs of the 21st century with a global economy and a longer living population are necessary. However, the fundamental tenet of an economically successful society balanced with justice, fairness and democracy remain.

Adopting a Social Democratic position also means that the SNP does not need to define itself in terms of where other parties stand. It does not need to be left or right of one, or more or less radical than another. It has its own philosophy to deal with issues and events. This allows it to act according to principles, rather than position itself with regard to where others are standing. It gives coherence for all the party's representatives, in whatever forum, to promote not just the cause of an Independent Scotland but a Social Democratic one.

It must also be a Party that not only seeks to administer in Devolution and take Scotland to Independence but aspires to govern it thereafter. It's not an alliance simply to deliver Independence then fragment into constituent parts, dissolving with members reforming in new or existing parties. It cannot end there. The role and duty of the Party is not simply to achieve Independence but deliver a prosperous, just and fair society thereafter.

In any event common sense dictates that it's British not Scottish parties that have the difficulties post Independence. Parties of Independence would welcome the new terrain but how do those who opposed it react. It's parties thirled to the British State that would have most trouble readjusting. It was Communist parties not Nationalist parties that needed to reinvent themselves when Independence followed the demise of the Soviet Union. It was nationalist not Unionist parties that formed the administrations in the Irish Free State and the Irish Republic. Unionist parties withered and died. Scotland will be no different.

For a Party with a stated philosophy and purpose there is as much work to do after Independence as before it. This is a Party not just for changing the constitutional position of Scotland but its social and economic situation. That means a coherent and stated aim not simply of an Independent Scotland but a just and fair one. It's an obligation to implement that programme. It would be absurd to hand over power in a newly independent land to those that had fought against it or opposed that social and economic vision. For supporters of a Social Democratic Scotland, the work is just beginning not ending on Independence Day. The myth that the SNP will fragment is just that, but it must be killed off. The SNP is not just for delivering an Independent Scotland but governing in an Independent Scotland.

As well as a coherent philosophy the Party needs to create a base in the community and achieve credibility in the Country. Successes, whether in northern Angus and Aberdeen or lowland Renfrewshire or West Lothian, have been based upon being part of the community and representing that locality in the political sphere. This is testament to their community roots not the loudness of their chorusing of Independence. The SNP has at times sought to lecture on the future merits of Independence rather than represent the immediate needs of the area. Both need apply as part of the general political philosophy and not just the route to electoral success.

Not simply as part of a modern Social Democratic ethos but historically, the SNP has been committed to subsidiarity and decisions being taken as close as possible to the communities they affect. This commitment to community involvement and the empowerment of individuals has been the basis of success at local government level and straddles the philosophy of the Party. Lessons must be learned from the winning areas. The basis for the Party is campaigning for Independence from within the community not championing it from without. The SNP as well as being a Social Democratic party must be Scotland's Party.

As well as being rooted in the community there must also be credibility within the Country. That means that its senior spokespeople and elected representatives must be able to articulate a clear vision of the society they seek and the Government they offer. They must be knowledgeable of the areas they cover and issues they converse on. They must also interact not simply with the parliamentary press but the trade and representative organisations. Providing a credible alternative not simply narrating a litany of Executive failures or a mantra chant of British faults. Too often the SNP is seen to oppose not to promote, to castigate not advocate. That must change. It is important in a democracy that an Opposition do the necessary job of challenging the Administration. It is equally important though that a Party that aspires to govern and seeks to Build a Nation outline their alternatives and vision. Scots are aware of the ineptitude of the Lib/Lab Executive; what they need persuaded of is the ability of the SNP.

Parties that aspire to govern never mind take a Nation to Independence must also have discipline both within and without. Recent internal difficulties within the Party have been well publicised. Divided parties do not win elections and the cause of Independence cannot be jeopardised by individual tantrums or petty petulance. Party harmony is best served when all members sign up to a clear political philosophy, which can be easily developed and applied to arising situations. The Party will be stronger when all stand on a strong political foundation that is clearly defined.

It's equally important to argue not only what you are in favour of, but also what you are not. Politics is about hard choices. Running a Country and building a Nation does not come easily. Difficult decisions need to be made and conflicting interests balanced and adjudicated on. The SNP cannot simply be in favour of everything and against nothing. Nor can it call for ever greater expenditure from a limited budget especially when improved results are either lacking or intangible. Discipline in policy as well as practice is required. Cheap soundbites or shabby electioneering undermine a coherent philosophy and generate electoral contempt. They belong to a party of protest not a party of government.

Abject poverty and unacceptable social conditions exist in Scotland. This is shameful for an oil rich country at the commencement of the twenty first century. Scotland though is not a Third World Nation. It is not a basket case destined for purgatory but a Nation that is underperforming and capable of doing so much more. The problem in Scotland is not that things are so bad but that they could be so much better. It is with a mixture of jealousy and frustration that Scots have looked on as other countries with fewer resources have achieved so much more. Small Nations of a comparable size whether Ireland or Finland have delivered so much more with so much less. Criticism should be targeted and appropriate, not scattergun and subject to hyperbole, no matter how good the soundbite or how clever the headline. The Party needs to build up Scottish self-confidence and create a desire to do better and achieve more, not create a mood of despair and despondency.

It's important that channels of communication be opened between parties, organisations and individuals with a shared commitment to Independence. Good relations can be cost free. However, it is not the only area in which co-operation can and should occur. Being seen to lead exclusively on the constitution would be highly damaging and reinforce the stereotypical perception of the Party. It must stand up for Scotland on all matters.

Being Scotland's Party means being prepared to lead and form coalitions and alliances on a variety of issues. These are not simply constitutional but social, economic and environmental. If the name and the perception amongst the electorate of being Scotland's Party are to be both worth having and lived up to then an inclusive attitude is needed. Too often the SNP has appeared as overtly strident if not politically sectarian. That has been damaging in the past and is inappropriate now. Scotland finds itself in a new political landscape. Not simply in Holyrood but also the Council chamber with proportional representation. Throughout the country a multi-party and no-party democracy has developed, partly as a result of the growth of fringe parties and partly as people turn off and away from all parties. The decline in electoral turnout has not been matched with a decline in political activity. It has simply recreated itself in new forms and different ways outwith the formal and established parties. Community activism has grown almost in direct comparison to the decline of formal political activity. That means establishing links in the community but working with, not imposing on, local groups and national organisations that are involved in that specific field. That must mean business interests as well protest groups. The economy is fundamental and championing that is pivotal. Fiscal autonomy can be won and the SNP must lead that campaign. While offering formal political leadership in Parliament and Council chambers as befits the largest opposition party in Scotland, and also working with others both within those Institutions and without, the Party must be seen as open and inclusive leading on a broad swathe of Scottish issues not simply promoting the cause of Independence.

Scotland's constitutional breakthrough in the referendum came as a result of a national agenda that change was needed and a Parliament was essential. It also applies in other areas. The social and economic successes of countries such as Sweden and Ireland were predicated on a national consensus. They recognised that unless common cause was made then aims could neither be realised nor goals reached whether in economic success or social harmony. Parties of a spectrum of political hues recognised that a national agenda transcended individual party interests. They subscribed to that both in power and in opposition. The UK has been afflicted by a political malaise of short-termism. The fall of an Administration is accompanied by a reversal in policy and direction. In any event Governments concentrate on immediate political advantage not long term national interest. Scotland cannot replicate the faults of the UK but must learn from the successes of other small Nations. There must be a long term national consensus on the economic direction and core values of the State. The Party whether in opposition or in power has a duty to seek, refine and uphold them.

In summary, the SNP needs to define itself as a mainstream European Social Democratic Party, representing the interests of the Country not simply the constitution. A Party rooted in the community and earning credibility across the Country. A Party committed to Building Scotland up not knocking Scotland down. Creating the best devolved Scotland there can be but offering so much more – the opportunity to Build a Nation.

CHAPTER 5

Scotland – Healthy, Wealthy and Wise?

'The test of our progress is not whether we add more to
the abundance of those who have much; it is whether
we provide enough for those who have too little'
Franklin D Roosevelt, 2 January 1937
(Second Inaugural Presidential Address)

THE SNP SEEKS TO Build a Nation with a vibrant economy and quality
social services. What's wrong with that? The two are not exclusive
but interdependent. Why should they be mutually irreconcilable as
opposed to being part and parcel of a just and fair society? Other
countries do it so why not Scotland. Labour criticises the Party for
seeking to do so by using a model of low Irish business taxes but
Swedish quality social services. The Tories parrot the criticism.
Whilst one lacks ambition for the Country the other lacks common
humanity for its People. It is, however, a charge that still has to be
answered.

It's a hard and competitive world in the new global economy.
There are no free lunches for countries and competition is growing
by the day. No-one owes a living to this small land of ours located
on the North West periphery of Europe. In a global economy competition comes not just from the eastern parts of the EU but from
the booming economies in the southern hemisphere. Whether in
trade or tourism Scotland needs to compete on a global basis. It is
blessed with many natural resources but it still requires to trade to
generate wealth. Action therefore needs taken to avoid slipping back-
wards never mind moving forwards. Without wealth creation social

services will at best disintegrate and at worst become a distant memory. The Swedish welfare state is founded on the strength of its economy, not just the humanity of its society. The success of its welfare state could not have been achieved without a strong economy and cannot be maintained in its absence. Economic success has allowed the Swedes fair shares of the cake not fair shares of misery.

So, why not have Swedish social services predicated on Swedish economic policies, if that is what you aspire to? Although alternative models can be considered, each Nation is unique. Whilst the Swedish social welfare model may have been possible in the past it is not an option now. Other factors such as the basis of the economy or geography also intervene. Even in the Scandic countries the arrival of the global economy accompanied by increased competition from the Accession States on the other side of the Baltic Sea is seeing them reconsider their fiscal policies. In Scotland's case, it's not simply global competition from those Accession States or Asia. Scotland is located on the same island as London and the rest of the UK economy. It is, also, situated across a narrow channel from low tax Ireland. A competitive edge is therefore needed to both retain existing jobs and recruit new ones. Why locate in Scotland when skills and resources are more readily available in London? Why high tax Scotland rather than low tax Ireland?

An example of a dynamic and vibrant economy is to be found by looking across the Irish Sea. Within a generation our Celtic cousins have overtaken us from a position far back at the time of their Independence. In the absence of North Sea oil they have left Scots as much in awe of their economic performance as they are of Swedish social services. The Irish learned that to compete and grow their economy they required to have a competitive edge. That edge cannot come from quality of life alone though Scotland possesses that in abundance, nor from simply being part of the Anglo-phone world. It must come from a distinct economic advantage. That means a competitive business tax regime. Bribes and inducements cannot compensate for an uncompetitive economic environment. That strategy has been tried and has failed. Whilst other Nations may also offer a competitive tax regime, additional factors whether quality of life or language can see you through. In its absence you are hamstrung from the start and on the sidelines of the global competition.

The global economy has also changed the role of the State with regard to the economy. Gone are the days of running major sectors of industry or micro managing the economy. The days of nationalisation of major industries have passed whether as a stop gap to closure or as the way of running them from the outset. That is not to deny the role of the State in the running of services whether social or otherwise. PFI and PPP in the NHS, education and other services have been a disaster. A hard lesson has been learnt not just in the railways but in energy with nuclear power. The global economy dictates that the days of nationalisation of the means of production are past. Clause 4 socialism is as redundant in the economy as it is in the Labour Party.

In the 1980s the SNP was involved in opposing factory closures whether at Plessey, Lee Jeans or BL Bathgate. When more recently closure came at Motorola no such action occurred. Neither because the closure was less catastrophic nor because the Party was less supportive of those afflicted but simply because nothing could be done. In the global economy owning the means of production alone is insufficient. Motorola would have offered the keys to the workforce, but if they couldn't sell mobile phones in a world market how could a workers co-op or a state industry. Even the absence of a profit margin would not have sold what would not be bought. The world has changed. In the new century knowledge and access to markets are more important than simply ownership of the means of production.

The role of the State in the 21st century economy is to provide the framework in skills and infrastructure upon which enterprise can develop; to promote the national interest and protect the rights of the citizen. It is not to run businesses or micro-manage the economy. The remit of the public and private sectors are distinct but complementary. There requires to be a proper 'public private partnership'. The State has clear duties in service provision.

It's not just a global economy but a knowledge economy. The State is pivotal in ensuring that the Nation can compete in both. Infrastructure improvements are necessary given Scotland's geography and topography. That applies as much to the electronic highway as to road and rail links. The nature of the modern economy means that knowledge is ever more essential. The pace and rapidity of change in communication, technology and science mean that not just the labour force but the Nation must be ahead of changes and developments that lead the economy. An essential aspect of that is not just a skilled workforce but an educated population. Specific skills and particular techniques may be the responsibility of the employer but an educated population able to learn and adapt in a fast changing world remains the duty of the State. Lessons must be learned from the Scandic Nations and Sweden in particular where participation rates for 18 year olds in education are almost double that of the UK.[1]

Providing the educated population needed in a knowledge economy; creating the transport and telecommunications networks required in a global one; delivering the quality public services needed for a just and fair society are all the duty of the State. It's not the role of the private sector to provide an educated workforce nor a transport or telecommunications network fit for purpose in the twenty first century. Market forces are not appropriate in public services. Schools and hospitals are for education and treatment not private profit. Undue regulation is unhelpful to a vibrant and dynamic economy. But regulation concerning health and safety, the environment, or employment is right and proper. Rather than

---

[1] Participation rates in education for 18 year olds:
Sweden: 95.5% Finland: 87.3% Norway: 86.6% UK: 55.5%
(Eurostat Year Book 2003)

detracting from commercial success it can enhance it and is in any event perfectly legitimate for a balanced society.

Competitive business taxation is not inconsistent with social justice and quality public services. It is in fact a prerequisite. It's a different way of growing public revenues not sacrificing public services. Low business taxes generate high public finances, as other countries have recognised. It's not placing the citizen's interest beneath that of the corporations but recognising that both are intertwined. Nokia's success is good for Finland, Ericsson's for Sweden and indeed the Royal Bank for Scotland. A healthy economy allows for healthy citizens. A low business tax regime can fuel the Scottish economy and provide the necessary funds without which nothing can be achieved.

A low business tax regime allied with a high quality of life and membership of the Anglophone community allows Scotland to seek to minimise the handicaps of its geography and maximise the benefits of it. From Super Port installations to renewable energy in abundance, Scotland's geography and climate offer an opportunity to turn adversity into advantage. Wind and wave once viewed with distaste and disdain offer clean energy in abundance. A location as the port of entry for Europe not its periphery is also possible. It's not simply in those sectors alone that opportunities arise but within the whole manufacturing base. Peripherality is ended and a competitive advantage acquired. That, however, is dependent on the economic factors underpinning the Country. These areas can see Scotland lift off economically but a low business tax regime fuels the engine.

While changes in business taxation have been brought about by the global economy, personal taxation has not remained immune from change. No one relishes paying tax and accordingly greater transparency is needed to show the link between services received and tax paid. A shift from hidden taxes to fair taxes is therefore required. Tax increases have been substantial over recent years but through indirect not direct taxation, the consequence of which is that the relationship between tax due and ability to pay is being eroded. A move away from that is both necessary and correct. Fair taxation is essential. A higher rate for higher earners is also fair and appropriate. However, the days of punitive taxation have gone. It must be proportionate. It must be transparent and it must be acceptable.

In a global economy not only is capital mobile but so are people. Free movement of labour is available within the EU along with job opportunities elsewhere whether in the Gulf or Australia. This means competition for skills. Punitive taxation would see the young and the talented move to competitor Nations. Those are the very people that Scotland must not only retain but attract. Given that high skills are vital for the economy, personal taxation can't be such that it causes relocation whether within the UK or Europe. That does not preclude fair tax and fair tax rates but recognises that the global economy exists for skills as well as jobs.

A vibrant economy is necessary for the well being of citizens as much as the well being of citizens is needed for the health of the economy. A quality welfare state adds to the quality of life provided by Scotland's natural environment. Other successful Nations are testimony to this. Sweden is ranked second only to her Scandic neighbour Norway in the United Nations Quality Of Life Index[2]. It's that quality of life that allows it to lead in economic areas such as the Competitiveness Index[3] putting Stockholm up with the world leaders along with her Scandic sister city of Helsinki. Economic growth brings quality of life and quality of life brings economic success. The two become a virtuous circle.

The strength of the Swedish economy and the merits of its

---

[2] UN Quality Of Life Index, UN Development Programme

[3] Rober Huggins Assc. European Competitiveness Index 2004 Top 5 regions are: Finland, Sweden, Belgium, France and Switzerland – Scotland currently features in position 42

quality of life are not only interlinked but are the bedrock of quality public services, which in turn are the foundations for prosperity for both Nation and citizen. That is reflected in the health, wealth and cohesion of its society. It has facilitated the provision of services addressing poverty and ill health that far surpass that afforded or provided in Scotland or the UK. They have not only provided for better treatment for the individual but created a better society for all their citizens. The statistics disclose, for example that Sweden has 60 per cent more doctors[4] and 50 per cent less poverty[5] than the UK.

But funds are not limitless. Infrastructure has also been neglected and must be addressed if Scotland is to overcome its current geographic disadvantage. Whether in the road or rail network or the modern broadband highway Scotland is behind many of its competitors. That requires to be addressed as a priority. However, simply spending more money does not necessarily equate with better services. The Executive trumpets higher than ever expenditure but the patient or council taxpayer just sees poorer services or facilities. There has to be a calling to account for the substantial funds being committed. Simply spending more is not necessarily available nor should it be acceptable. The public sector as much as the private sector must provide value for money.

That said, there is work to be done, limited budget or not. There are shameful social problems to address as a matter of urgency in Scotland. Poverty, poor housing and appalling health statistics abound. At the start of the new millennium they are unacceptable in

---

[4] Number of doctors per 100,000 inhabitants:
Sweden: 283; Denmark: 317; Norway: 280; Netherlands: 311; UK: 176.
(Eurostat Year Book 2003)

[5] The risk of poverty is the percentage of people with a disposable income below the 'risk of poverty' threshold – which is set at 60pc of national median disposable income.
In Sweden, 10% of the population are at risk of poverty;
Denmark, 9%; Netherlands, 12%; Across Europe, 17%; UK, 21%.
(Eurostat Year Book 2003)

an oil rich society. How though are they to be remedied? Scotland is also a changing society. Demographic trends mean that there is a decreasing working population but an increasing elderly one. The tax base is shrinking but medical and scientific research is growing and ensuring greater longevity for the human race. Put simply, fewer are working but more are claiming. The amount that could be spent on health in particular is limitless but funds are not infinite.

The assumption in social democracy had been that high taxation would see redistribution of wealth and the provision of universal benefits for all. An informal social contract was entered into whereby higher earners contributed through tax but received through benefits. Demographic changes, attitudes to tax and a global economy have broken that contract. In these changed circumstances, universality of each and every benefit is unsustainable. Scotland is not alone in undergoing this review. All western democracies face this challenge. Even in Sweden it is under consideration. That doesn't mean abandoning responsibilities but it does mean addressing priorities.

There are fundamental tenets that must be upheld and universal benefits that must be provided. The weakest must always be cared for and the most vulnerable protected. The shameful poverty that scars this land must be addressed and the elderly who provided for us must be cared for. Those must be the imperatives.

A universal health service available to all and free at the point of delivery is a fundamental tenet of a Social Democratic society and must be provided. That though does not mean that every cosmetic operation must be funded or every consumer choice pandered to. Arguing for that is to either write a blank cheque or simply ensure fair shares of suffering all round. To maximise the benefits of the advancement of medical science and to ensure its provision to all, in some instances those who can afford to pay should make some contribution. That is not irreconcilable with free basic care but ensures the maximum availability of the latest advances and medicines. An unlimited budget cannot be provided for a limitless service.

An equal pillar of a just a fair society is that care must be provided from the cradle to the grave. In sickness and in health, from childhood to old age, certain fundamental tenets again remain the duty of the State. Universal childcare, a citizens' income, and a dignified old age pension are all absolutes for such a society.

Some social and economic benefits go hand in hand. Universal childcare allows people to return to the labour market. It addresses child poverty that is at scandalous levels in Scotland. A citizens' income makes for a productive labour force. It provides a decency threshold below which no citizen can fall. An integrated tax and benefit structure is needed to end the poverty trap of a low wage economy coupled with an anachronistic system. Other measures are simply taken because they are right and proper. A society is judged not by how it treats those who are strongest and most powerful within it but how it provides for the weakest and most vulnerable. Providing a fit and proper pension for all in this land who have contributed so much to its creation is essential. There must be dignity as well as respect in old age.

Meeting those commitments from eradicating child poverty to ending penury in old age is unquestionable. They must, therefore, be universal and unchallengable. There are, however, other matters to which universality cannot be applied. Universal benefits across the board would be financially unsustainable. Finite resources must be used to maximum effect. Choices outwith those areas must be made. The responsibility of the State is to protect the vulnerable not subsidise the wealthy. Are free school breakfasts for those in need not a better means of addressing poverty than free school lunches for those who can well afford it? Are free eye tests for all best use of public funds for those who are buying designer frames? Is the dignity of a fair and decent pension not preferable to piecemeal handouts for pensioners? Priorities must be chosen but responsibilities must be maintained.

A vibrant economy and quality public services are not mutually exclusive but interlinked. They are equally necessary for a fair and just society. Simply creating wealth does not automatically lead to a prosperous society. Economic indicators on their own are not testament to a Nation's well being. A society requires cohesion as well as competitiveness. The wealth created must be spent wisely and distributed widely. The alternative model to Sweden championed by many is that of the United States, however, the enviable economic statistics of the USA must be juxtaposed with shameful social statistics. From child poverty to gun crime it is not a model that Scotland should copy.

Changes in taxation are only one of the measures required. Tax should not be punitive but it should be redistributive. A higher rate of tax for higher earners is right and proper. Societies that are financially hugely divided are inherently unstable providing a breeding ground for crime and other social ills. It's not about eliminating the wealthy but eradicating poverty. Personal wealth is perfectly acceptable but abject poverty is not. A Nation's wealth cannot simply be measured in the individual income or collective riches of its citizens but by a myriad of factors which cannot be measured in monetary terms alone. Their absence carries a social cost that is immeasurable.

None of this is new to Scotland. Post war an economy required to be rebuilt and infrastructure provided. But, it was married to the creation of the welfare state in which key responsibilities were met. That was done through prioritising the economy and prioritising those services to be provided. Investment in the economy and in infrastructure allowed for a fight against poverty and care for the elderly. A new Scotland and a just Scotland were the post war goals to be achieved through regeneration of the economy and provision of infrastructure together with care for the young and the old. Times have changed as has the economy and the way in which services are provided. The State is less and communities and individuals are more but the ambitions should remain. Low business taxes and quality social services are not mutually exclusive but absolutely essential in Building a Nation that is wealthy, healthy and wise.

CHAPTER 6

Independence in Europe – Nothing Less

'Europe represents a contribution toward a better world'
Jean Monnet

INDEPENDENCE IN EUROPE HAS been SNP policy for many years and rightly so. It was a necessary political change to end the perceived difficulties of separatism and isolation. It provided a bridge to Independence across the turbulent waters from the Union. It brought about a coherent political philosophy that was outward looking and internationalist as opposed to introspective and isolationist.

However, the EU has changed and evolved beyond all recognition over recent years. It now finds itself at a historic juncture. Is it a United States of Europe or is it a Europe of Nation States? It is not simply monetary union and eastward expansion but the very purpose of the organisation that is ongoing and under review. In many instances changes have occurred with lightning speed and go further and faster than the current will and understanding of the peoples of Europe. Within a short space of time Europe has begun to creep into aspects of life previously viewed as sacrosanct to the Nation State. It is not simply the abolition of border posts and currencies but regulation in trivial aspects of day to day life that have occurred. The debate is not peculiar to Scotland, or the need to adapt unique to the SNP. These difficulties afflict most parties not simply within the UK but across Europe. The debate about the future of Europe is ongoing.

In Scotland, the Institution has come into disrepute and downright contempt, sometimes falsely over alleged regulations on bagpipe playing, other times quite correctly over the destruction of our fishing fleet. Fundamentally, though, many of the ills in Scotland have been the failures of British representation than the flaws in European actions. From fishing to social funds it has been poor UK representation or a failure to represent Scottish interests not a prejudice in Brussels against our small land. Changes are happening and will continue to happen in Europe. The choices are made not by Regional Governments, but by Nation States. Independence is necessary or any policy is academic. But, assuming it's achieved, what of the policy of Independence in Europe? Does the SNP veer away from support for independent membership of the EU or does it argue for a vision of a social and economic union based on Independent Nation States?

For both the SNP and Scotland Independence in Europe must remain both the route to and the vision of an Independent Scotland. The EU despite its many criticisms and numerous faults remains an organisation that has transformed the continent of Europe for the better and offers the prospect not just of an economically vibrant community but a socially harmonious one. The Union after all is social as well as economic. It is and will continue to undergo great change but it is for Scotland to be within the Institution arguing for the changes it seeks, not to be outwith marginalised and powerless. In addition, it is the only credible route by which Scotland will become independent. Independence outwith Europe may be theoretically possible but it remains politically unrealisable.

It cannot, though, be membership at any price or on any terms. Criticism of the centralisation of the EU is not indicative of opposition to membership. It is in fact to align with the majority of the small Nations in the EU who seek the benefits of co-operation whilst retaining their Independence and freedom. The Scandic countries and many others do not seek to be integrated into a Franco-German alliance. Nor do they wish to be dominated and dictated to by Brussels on each and every issue. The new Accession States have in many instances only recently obtained their Independence and freedom of action. They have no wish to be assimilated into a European super state. Instead they seek a relationship built on fields of responsibility. Retaining a Nation State's sovereign powers of decision making including the right to cede certain powers for collective action on areas best dealt with on a transnational basis.

Brussels deciding and regulating on all aspects of life from the ingredients of a sausage to the shape of a banana is absurd. They may have been apocryphal but were symptomatic of a perception of an all pervasive Europe. The widening of the EU has ensured that it will not be deepened or certainly not for a long time to come. Membership is on the basis of supporting an EU of Nation States not a Federal States of Europe. It is not a centralised Europe but a Europe of Nations. It is Independence in Europe.

The EU has evolved over generations from an original coal and steel community through the EEC to the social and economic union that it is today. It has done so on a continent that for centuries was plagued by war and strife and at the end of the last millennium saw two world wars reap carnage not just on combatants but civilians. If nothing else the evolution of a European community has put an end to war in much of Europe and ended centuries old antagonisms and enmities bringing co-operation where once there was conflict. For that alone the EU is to be supported.

But it is more than that. It has brought down the barriers between States and expanded the borders of Europe. Neither Germany nor Europe is now divided by the Oder Neisser line. The Iron Curtain that descended on post war Europe has been consigned to the history books. A generation is growing in a Europe of opportunity not oppression. That too is an undoubted boon not just for individuals but many Nation States that were caught in the crossfire of the Cold War.

Travel across the Continent and within the EU is particular has been freed up and made significantly easier, benefiting not just trade and tourism but the relationship between peoples and States. From school exchanges to package holidays, meeting and mixing has shrunk the distance and narrowed the divide between the peoples of Europe. The Schengen agreement offers up the chance for passport-less travel. That can only be a good thing.

However, it is much more than that. It is the basis of Scottish trade and commercial interests. The Scottish economy is not just dependent on trade with our larger neighbour south of the border but with our trading partners on the European Continent. The large economies of France and Germany are important but so are expanding ones in the Accession States. Economic prosperity is dependent on retaining access to those markets and membership offers that opportunity as well as other benefits. Scotland is inextricably linked economically and will remain so.

The question of whether Scotland would become a member of the EU on Independence has been well canvassed. Suffice to say that in addition to sound legal arguments, real politic indicates that membership will occur. There is precedent whether in Greenland's difficulties in extricating itself from Danish membership or the automatic acceptance of a unified Germany. Fundamentally at a time when Europe is still seeking to expand why would it wish to contract? Why would Croatia be welcomed and Scotland shunned? Why would the EU seek to eject or reject its major energy provider never mind its valuable international waters? Scotland will be able to join the EU and suggestions to the contrary are spurious.

But, why not Independence outwith Europe? Why not recognise the benefits of the EU but access in from without or do so from another sphere? There are those who wish to see an Independent Scotland be just that and refuse to cede powers and sovereignty to any body and certainly not the EU. Others prefer to see Scotland look west, seeking to trade with the USA rather than the EU. Still others seek a special relationship similar to that possessed by Norway. None of them are possible, practical or desirable. Independence outwith the EU may be theoretically possible but it is not politically practical.

All Nations are both Independent and Interdependent. A multitude of factors but in particular the global economy has ensured that it is so. Unless you seek to replicate North Korea or Albania then interaction is required. The global economy is seeing the creation of major trading blocs whether in Europe, the American continent or South East Asia. The logical one for Scotland formed both from trading alliances and social perspectives is to align with Europe. Not just Scotland's economy but much of her social perspectives are in tune and harmony with the European not transatlantic model. From the rights of citizens to the duty of the State; from war in Vietnam to conflict in the Gulf, Scotland has greater affinity with European colleagues than Atlantic cousins. Scotland is a European Nation not the 51st state. It's a social and economic union not NAFTA for us. A siege economy will never appeal to the electorate and the disruption and dislocation that would be caused by seeking to leave the EU make it electorally disastrous. As membership minimises the fears of disruption and dislocation leaving it would maximise it.

The final option argued for by some is to leave the EU and seek a special relationship akin to that of Norway. That may have been possible in the past but is highly unlikely now. The Norwegian situation is an historical anachronism, created when the EU was a vastly different and smaller organisation. It was based on the general assumption that Norway will join at some time in the future. New members of the EU such as the Czech Republic and Poland or existing members such as Ireland and Finland would be highly unlikely to agree to any special deal. Membership would undoubtedly be on offer but it would be on the same terms and conditions that were imposed on them. No more and no less. Why would they confer the benefits of membership without the cost of joining it? Why would they give a better deal to us than they have themselves?

They might not be able to amend the Norwegian relationship but it is certain that the rules of membership to be granted to Scotland would be those that applied to all others not another special case. Stay in or stay out, but on the rules that apply for all member not one special case.

But it's not just the Europe we oppose that needs to be identified, but the Europe we seek that needs to be explained. It as an opportunity to build a vision not just of Scotland as it can be but Europe as it should be. The EU post Maastricht is after all both a social and economic union irrespective of opt outs and delays sought and invoked by Thatcher. It offers an opportunity for collective action by Nation States against many social failings.

The EU is not a European version of the US. It offers far more and indeed is a bulwark to much that emanates from that seemingly omnipotent Nation. A social union offers an opportunity to level up not down. The SNP must argue positively for the EU and what it can be as it argues for an Independent Scotland and all it should be. There has been an historic opposition to the concept of the EU from much of the Left both in Scotland and in the UK. That has not and should not be replicated by the SNP. Social Democratic parties in Europe have looked on perplexed as those on the Left in Britain have denounced it as a Capitalist club. But why should Europe simply be a free market and not a just and fair society? The strength of the EU is not simply in its economic, but also in its social opportunities. The arguments for accepting the case for and from a left perspective have been outlined before lucidly by David Purdy in *Eurovision or American Dream?*. The EU offers not just a bulwark against Atlanticisation but an opportunity to achieve the collective action that is needed. The SNP must oppose a European Super State but champion a Europe that is a social and economic union based on Nation States.

The same applies to the Euro. Membership of that offers not just economic but social advantages for Scotland. Better opportunities for manufacturers and lower interest rates for homeowners would be welcomed. It, also, has political advantages for the SNP avoiding the difficult situation of an Independent Scotland either remaining part of sterling or creating a separate currency. Both are possible but both have practical and significant political problems. For the SNP, like Scotland, membership of the Euro is best. In any event, membership of the Euro even for the UK is not a matter of if but when. It will be a commercial reality in a global world. Better to go in at the right rate seeking to maximise the advantages than to be dragged in grudgingly and belatedly. As an economy more dependent on trade than that of the UK its absence is felt harder in Scotland. Membership must, of course be at the right rate for the Scottish economy but membership there must be. The SNP should be supportive of that. The Euro is good for Scots and the Scottish economy.

Independence in Europe remains as valid now as in the past. It requires to be updated to take account of the new EU that has evolved. Opposition to a super state must be made clear but co-operation for a social and economic union must be championed. It remains the only route by which Independence can be achieved and offers an opportunity for Nations to work collectively for the common wealth. Building a Europe of Nation States with a social and economic agenda.

CHAPTER 7

Taking Responsibility: how the Scots should see themselves

'A country of fearful men proud in the talking, paltry
in the living, and every promise another lie'
Andrew O'Hagan, *Our Fathers*

SCOTLAND NEEDS TO TAKE political, fiscal and social responsibility. Political responsibility to decide whether war is waged in our name or our fishing industry abandoned by our representatives. Fiscal responsibility to ensure that there is a Parliament that recognises that it must generate wealth before it can spend it. Social responsibility to recognise that many problems in modern Scotland are self-inflicted and that the cure comes from within. Such responsibilities need to be exercised both collectively by Scotland as a Nation and individually by Scots as citizens. For too long, Scots have been unwilling to accept responsibility for their society. The excuses and blame must cease and the action and cures begin.

Scotland does not have its problems to seek. It has too often blamed them all on others or on circumstances. That is not the case and must cease. From a denial that problems exist to the excuse that it is all the fault of the Union denies the reality. Some do come from the consequences of the Union. Many lie rooted in poverty. Many, though, do not. Thatcherism caused pain and massive social dislocation, damaging individuals and fracturing communities. Mass unemployment resulted and urban ghettos were created. They became a breeding ground for social problems. Her guilt should neither be exonerated nor lessened in any way.

Other social problems abound in Scotland that can neither directly nor indirectly be laid at the door of Thatcherism. Blaming it on her or suggesting that a big boy did it and ran away denies that the responsibility and resolution lies with us. From binge drinking to a deep-fried Mars bar diet and from domestic violence to a knife culture, there are aspects of our society that are wrong and flawed. They emanate from problems that lie within not without. For too long in Scotland, too many excuses have been made. But it's not the recognition of the cause but the identification of the solution that is needed. The arrival of the Parliament means that Scotland must take responsibility for its social problems and solving them.

Access to fresh fruit and vegetables are pricey for many but a deep-fried Mars bar and Buckfast culture is equally costly for society. Poverty may be a breeding ground for crime, but domestic violence is longstanding in a country that venerates machismo. Violence is rooted in social problems but in a society that tacitly enjoys the Scottish hard man image, what else is to be expected.

Other countries have taken a long hard look at themselves and addressed their cultural problems and social failings. The Finns held the sick man of Europe title prior to being surpassed by Scotland. Not just practical actions on food but social changes in alcohol and activity were encouraged. The Irish soon discovered that crime was not another legacy of British imperialism but a social problem that afflicted them as others; hence the creation of the Garda to replace the RIC. Other countries have changed and so must Scotland. The excuses must stop. The behaviour of individuals not just the attitude of the Nation needs addressed.

As well as the Nation taking responsibility so must the individual. Some of the social ills come from a cultural attitude others though are from the actions of individuals. A knife, Buckfast and deep-fried Mars bar culture are national problems borne from individual actions. A culture may create them it but its individuals who perpetrate them. Poor housing conditions are an indictment on our society but it is no excuse for anti-social behaviour. Respecting your stair or your neighbour's rights is not too much to expect. The extent of poverty in this land is shameful but that is no excuse for stealing from your neighbour or anyone else for that matter.

Social Democracy does not mean accepting bad behaviour just because it has a social explanation. It means: addressing the social and economic causes as well as the actions; providing the opportunities for individuals to better and improve themselves; and addressing the deeper rooted cultural attitudes that cause or feed such behaviour. Creating a new Scotland requires a change in attitudes as well as outcomes. It's not just about giving people rights but expecting them to accept responsibilities. It's about mutual respect, acknowledging the rights of others and a responsibility to the State as well as its duties to you.

It's not just how we are but how we see ourselves. It's a big world out there. England is our nearest neighbour and as a result of many social and economic links will remain hugely important for Scotland. However, it is not the beginning and end of the world just a major aspect of it. Scots need to stop defining themselves solely against the English and need to lose their hang-ups about their English cousins.

They are not intent on oppressing the Scots or of forcibly maintaining us in a Union. The political situation remains because the Scots allow it not because the English enforce it. The solution is to change the attitude of the Scots not condemn the English. In any event England is changing. Far from oppressing the Scots, most English frankly don't care. The social and demographic changes have transformed society south of the border. The number of immigrants and expansion in the south of the country have lessened age-old ties. Immigration will increase those trends. England is very much a multicultural society and resident Scots are but a small part. Social and demographic changes accompanied by greater integration with Europe result in many in England having more in common with

Brussels than Bathgate and being as likely to visit Lille as Loch Lomond. To many their kith and kin are across the channel or another sea rather than beyond the Solway and the Tweed.

The resurrection of English Nationalism whether through the support for their National sporting teams or flying of the flag of St George is a good thing. The English are rediscovering and re-claiming their own nationality. They are as uncomfortable with an artificial British identity as the Scots. The Union and the Empire pro-vided a unitary State and common purpose. The common identity it created has become outdated in post war Britain. A Great Britain Olympic team no more creates a Nation than does a British and Irish Lions Rugby team nor a European Ryder Cup Golf team. There are great similarities between the Scots and the English with huge overlaps in interests and attitudes, friendships and marriage. However, the respective national identities remain unique and do so through choice as much as circumstance. The arrival of the Scottish Parliament sees Scotland further defined as a different country albeit on a common island. Independence will add to rather than detract from the relationship.

Scots must end the victim culture and their perceived inferiority complex with their English cousins. They must cease defining themselves simply in comparison with that land. What happens there is important but not all-important. Often replicating them may be correct but in many instances it won't. The societies are diverging. The growth of huge urban conurbations makes English society considerably different from small town and small city Scotland. After all, England has a population ten times greater than Scotland's. The whole point of Devolution is an acknowledgement that the two Nations are unique, and different solutions are required for distinct problems.

Ireland underwent a similar transition. For many years not-withstanding Independence it still lived in the shadow of its former colonisers. Life and attitudes were defined by it. But a change evolved, even in a land scarred by poverty and afflicted by emigration. Factors as varied as the election of Mary Robinson as President to the success of Jack Charlton and their football team brought about a feeling of self-confidence and responsibility. A new generation grew up troubled not by the British past but seeing the possibilities of a European future. They have moved on from West Brits to Irish Europeans. Defining themselves by who they are not who they are not. Displaying confidence in themselves and ambitious for their country. The Scots must change likewise.

The problem in Scotland afflicts Unionists as much as Nationalists. This is shown in the perennial debate when a sporting occasion sees Scotland absent but England represented. Consternation strikes the land as inner soul searching commences. Who are Scots to support? Why should Scots either all support England or all pray for its elimination? It should be up to the individual. Those with an affinity or kin south of the Border may choose to support England and are entitled to do so. Others may choose another team depending on family ties or any other logical or whimsical choice. It is entirely up to them. To suggest that all English support Scotland and must do so is absurd. Those with an ethnic background from outwith the UK are more likely to see their second team reflected in Cyprus or Pakistan than a small Nation on the Celtic fringe. It doesn't and shouldn't matter who you chose to support: it's based on affinity not the Union. Similarly though Scots must cease getting vicarious pleasure from English defeats. It's Scotland's successes we should celebrate not English losses. This eternal debate is testimony to a lack of confidence in simply being Scottish.

Changes in Scottish attitudes are also needed in terms of welcoming success and supporting wealth creation. For too long a 'kent is faither' syndrome has been prevalent and festered. The support to rise so high but go no further, to do well but not to excel, to shine, but not too brightly. This attitude is unacceptable. It's churlish and damaging. The denigration of success and successful Scots must cease. What's good for them is good for Scotland. This is a national malaise and indicative of a society lacking in self-confidence. As with most cultural changes a simple legislative change is not available. It requires to be acknowledged, challenged and ultimately changed.

It's ironic that such a destructive attitude should prevail in a Nation that venerated education, promoted self-improvement and was the home of the Enlightenment. Success abroad was laudable, but success at home becomes a liability. In Scotland a legacy of a municipal socialist culture is both a curse and a blessing. It sees success as likely to be castigated as praised. It allows many to succeed who might otherwise have failed. Success is to be within limits; so high but no further. Artistic expression is promoted but stardom cut down. Education is fostered but intellect despised. Prosperity is sought but wealth condemned.

In Scotland, rags turned to riches can mean respect turned to resentment. Scottish society is littered with tales of the 'lad o'pairts' being cast asunder. From movie stars to sporting heroes none are exempt from castigation. The greatest vilification, though, is reserved for the entrepreneur. In the global economy wealth creation is vital. Scots who are pivotal in it deserve to be praised not pilloried. In Ireland the Michael O'Learys and Dermot Desmonds are seen as bringing wealth to the Nation and benefiting one and all. That is not replicated in Scotland but must be. It does not mean fawning sycophancy or a worshipping of wealth. Nor does it mean excusing bad behaviour or courting avarice. It is simply recognition of a valid and important contribution to society. It's an attitude that afflicts companies as much as individuals. The success of the Royal Bank of Scotland and other corporations has been good news bringing jobs and prosperity. If they pay their taxes, treat their staff well and grow the economy they should be supported.

Scotland must move on. To do so it must recognise not just the need to take political and fiscal responsibility but also social responsibility. To be confident in being Scottish; making this land all it can be not harking back and blaming others for our ills. Recognising that faults lie within as well as without. Being prepared to challenge cultural mores as well as the constitutional settlement. Challenging the Scots as well as standing up for Scotland. Welcoming not belittling success. Not being aggrieved and bitter North Brits but confident and outward looking Scottish Europeans. The Nation needs to be built on solid foundations.

CHAPTER 8

Who are the Scots – Are we all Jock Tamson's bairns?

'That man to man the warld o'er
Shall brothers be for a' that'

Robert Burns

'AW JOCK TAMSON'S BAIRNS' – a euphemism used by Scots for an egalitarian society, but does it reflect modern Scotland? Immigration is a global phenomenon of the twenty first century and Scotland has an ageing population. It's not only a fact of life but economically and socially necessary, as well as being culturally desirable. Immigration and immigrants should, therefore, be welcomed. The stereotypical red headed Scot is a myth. The Scots are a mongrel race formed by migrations throughout the millennia and over the centuries. That is a mixture of which we should be proud not ashamed. People have come from the first arrival of the Celts. They have travelled from across the Irish Sea, the European continent and the Indian subcontinent. From around the globe they have created the land that Scotland has become and this diversity must continue.

The Scottish Parliament must have powers over immigration but Scots also need to address their attitude to immigrants. The Fresh Talent initiative is well intentioned but flawed. The current incarceration of asylum seekers is a disgrace. Distinct powers are needed for a different society. It's not just about the economy but common humanity. The Scots and their Parliament must be able to address both their social and economic needs and meet their international and humanitarian obligations.

However, all Jock Tamson's bairns we are not. Recent deaths

and tragic events have shown that to be a myth. Racism is not an English disease but a social problem that afflicts Scotland as it does other lands. Scotland has to work at welcoming new migrants as it did to overcome prejudice against old ones. Sectarianism still blights Scottish society but less so than before and prejudice against Poles or Italians has lessened as they have become accepted as part of the community. No-one would quibble with the Scottishness of the Irish or Lithuanian communities or dispute the ethnicity of Sir Sean Connery. The Scottish Asian communities are now a distinct aspect of Scottish society. Socially, economically and culturally they have weaved a new pattern into the rich tapestry that is Scottish identity.

An increased effort is needed for those from new lands, many with a different racial origin or cultural background. Whether refugees from oppression or economic migrants they must be made welcome. Scots kith and kin set sail from Greenock or Cork for a better life in a new world. To now reject those who aspire likewise is unacceptable. Migrating to improve your life is not a crime. Scots and Scottish communities throughout the globe are testament to the contribution they make and the benefits they bring.

Those who come from south of the Border must be equally accepted. Whether they chose to come from Delhi or Dagenham should make no difference. Most English people who chose to move to Scotland permanently do so because they wish to live in a different land not to change it into their former land. The attitudes of a small minority are simply that. Their actions are no different from the behaviour of a minority of Scots elsewhere. Similarly, those who are only here to study or for a brief secondment for work can no more be expected to renounce their nationality than a Scot working elsewhere in the world. As our largest neighbour inward migration from England is inevitable. It is in any event ongoing. It should be welcomed rather than opposed. There can be no room for racism in Scotland against any peoples or country.

It is as valid and correct for immigrants to seek to maintain their culture as it is for Scots who have departed. Caledonian Clubs throughout the globe do not undermine the society in which they are formed but contribute to its diversity. Those who wish to maintain their own culture add to a new Scotland and do not undermine it. Canada is an example of what can be achieved. A land to which many Scots have migrated has shown what a boon immigration can be. The arrival of new Canadians from the Indian sub continent has contributed as much to Canadian identity as our own kith and kin. Chinatown in Vancouver and Little Italy in Toronto are as much part of Canadian society as the maple leaf or the pipe band from Nova Scotia. Far from eroding Canadian identity they have added to it. Without them assimilation into a greater USA would have been more likely. The same applies in Scotland.

Being Scottish is not exclusive but inclusive. It's not whether your forefathers fought at Bannockburn or fell at Culloden, nor is it whether you are white or Christian. It's about whether you reside here, recognise this as your home and wish to contribute to this community; along with adding to the distinctive identity that is being Scottish whether you have come from south of the border or from far further lands. The hands of many cultures and peoples from many lands will Build the Nation.

CHAPTER 9

Where now for Scotland and the SNP?

We're through with tokenism and gradualism and
see-how-far-you've-comeism. We're through with
we've-done-more-for-your-people-than-any-one elseism.
We can't wait any longer. Now is the time.
Martin Luther King

THE SCOTTISH NATION HAS existed for near on a thousand years. It had to fight for its Independence and its very existence. It has survived war and adversity. Its people have endured emigration and eviction. Yet the flames of Nationhood have been maintained. The incorporation into an Imperial Union diminished but could never extinguish them. An opportunity now arises to once more burn brightly on the world stage.

For too long Scots have built other Nations in far flung lands or remained at home to look on with envy at how much other Nations have achieved with far less. It is now time to be successful in our own land. Our Parliament, absent for 300 years, has been restored. Post Devolution there has been disappointment but the new building offers a fresh start.

The initial disappointments will be overcome and the mistakes rectified. The way forward will be incremental, building up both the Parliament as an Institution and the powers to be exercised within it. The relationship with England will require specific and unique solutions given the geography of the island. A new political culture will develop as will a new Scotland with immigration. It will be more self-confident and will move on.

The role of the SNP will be pivotal. It was the existence of the

SNP that drove and ultimately delivered Devolution. In the absence of a Party campaigning for Independence then its arrival will be far more difficult and far from assured. However, post Devolution the Party must reflect the new political landscape. It must nurture and support the Institution. It must have a social and economic profile as well as a constitutional one. It must be the Party of Independence, with a defined Social Democratic ethos.

As a Party it must be based in the community and credible with the public. It must espouse Social Democracy but recognise the effects of a global economy, never mind demographic changes. It must focus on a creating prosperity and delivering a just and fair society. It must run the devolved Parliament better, but more than that, it must show that Independence is the route to our Nation's prosperity, confidence and self-improvement.

Scotland needs to take political, fiscal and social responsibility, both individually and collectively. It requires fiscal freedom and Independent representation within the EU and the United Nations.

Post Devolution Nationalism is about Building our Nation.

Some other books published by **LUATH** PRESS
published from Scotland read around the world

Scotlands of the Future: sustainability in a small nation

Introduced and edited by Eurig Scandrett
ISBN 1 84282 035 4   PB   £7.99

What sorts of futures are possible for Scotland?

How can citizens of a small nation at the periphery of the global economy make a difference?

Can Scotland's economy be sustainable?

How do we build a good quality of life without damaging others'?

Could there be an economy that is good for people and the environment?

And if so, how do we get there without damaging people's livelihoods?

What can the Scottish Parliament do?

What difference can we make in our organisations, our trade unions, and our businesses?

Scotlands of the Future looks at where we've got to, where we can go next, and where we might want to get to – essential reading for those who think about and want to take action for a sustainable Scotland, and anyone else who cares about the future.

The anti-slavery campaigners succeeded. Politicians and civil society must rise to this new challenge, which is just today's version of the same injustice. We must show imagination, courage and leadership and champion a sustainable economy – for Scotland and the world.

OSBERT LANCASTER, EXECUTIVE DIRECTOR, CENTRE FOR HUMAN ECOLOGY

Eurovision or American Dream? Britain, the Euro and the Future of Europe

David Purdy
ISBN 1 84282 036 2   PB   £3.99

Should Britain join the euro?

Where is the European Union going?

Must America rule the world?

Eurovision or American Dream? assesses New Labour's prevarications over the euro and the EU's deliberations about its future against the background of transatlantic discord. Highlighting the contrasts between European social capitalism and American free market individualism, David Purdy shows how Old Europe's welfare states can be renewed in the age of the global market. This, he argues, is essential if European governments are to reconnect with their citizens and revive enthusiasm for the European project. It would also enable the EU to challenge US hegemony, not by transforming itself into a rival superpower, but by championing an alternative model of social development and changing the rules of the global game.

In this timely and important book David Purdy explains why joining the euro is not just a question of economics, but a question about the future political direction of Britain and its place in Europe. PROFESSOR ANDREW GAMBLE, DIRECTOR, POLITICAL ECONOMY RESEARCH CENTRE, DEPARTMENT OF POLITICS, UNIVERSITY OF SHEFFIELD

Scotland – Land and Power the agenda for land reform

Andy Wightman
in association with
Democratic Left Scotland
foreword by Lesley Riddoch
ISBN 0 946487 70 7   PB   £5.00

What is land reform?

Why is it needed?

Will the Scottish Parliament really make a difference?

Scotland – Land and Power argues passionately that nothing less than a radical, comprehensive programme of land reform can make the difference that is needed. Now is no time for palliative solutions which treat the symptoms and not the causes.

Scotland – Land and Power is a controversial and provocative book that clarifies the complexities of landownership in Scotland. Andy Wightman explodes the myth that land issues are relevant only to the far flung fringes of rural Scotland, and questions mainstream political commitment to land reform. He presents his own far-reaching programme for change and a pragmatic, inspiring vision of how Scotland can move from outmoded, unjust power structures towards a more equitable landowning democracy.

Writers like Andy Wightman are determined to make sure that the hurt of the last century is not compounded by a rushed solution in the next. This accessible, comprehensive but passionately argued book is quite simply essential reading and perfectly timed – here's hoping Scotland's legislators agree.
LESLEY RIDDOCH

Old Scotland New Scotland

Jeff Fallow
ISBN 0 946487 40 5 PB £6.99

Together we can build a new Scotland based on Labour's values. DONALD DEWAR, Party Political Broadcast

Despite the efforts of decent Mr Dewar, the voters may yet conclude they are looking at the same old hacks in brand new suits.

IAN BELL, THE INDEPENDENT

At times like this you suddenly realise how dangerous the neglect of Scottish history in our schools and universities may turn out to be.
MICHAEL FRY, THE HERALD

...one of the things I hope will go is our chip on the shoulder about the English... The SNP has a huge responsibility to articulate Scottish independence in a way that is pro-Scottish and not anti-English.
ALEX SALMOND, THE SCOTSMAN

Scottish politics have never been more exciting. In *Old Scotland New Scotland* Jeff Fallow takes us on a graphic voyage through Scotland's turbulent history, from earliest times through to the present day and beyond. This fast-track guide is the quick way to learn what your history teacher didn't tell you, essential reading for all who seek an understanding of Scotland and its history.

Eschewing the romanticisation of his country's past, Fallow offers a new perspective on an old nation.

Too many people associate Scottish history with tartan trivia or outworn romantic myth. This book aims to blast that stubborn idea.
JEFF FALLOW

A Passion for Scotland

David R. Ross
ISBN 1 84282 019 2 PB £5.99

David R. Ross is passionate about Scotland's past. And its future. In this heartfelt journey through Scotland's story, he shares his passion for what it means to be a Scot.

Eschewing xenophobia, his deep understanding of how Scotland's history touches her people shines through. All over Scotland, into England and Europe, over to Canada, and the United States – the people and the places that bring Scotland's story to life and death, are here. Included are the:

- Early Scots
- Wallace and Bruce
- The Union
- Montrose
- The Jacobites
- John MacLean
- Tartan Day USA

and, revealed for the first time, the burial places of all Scotland's monarchs.

This is not a history book, but it covers history.

This is not a travel guide, but some places mentioned might be worth a visit.

This is not a political manifesto, but a personal one.

Read this book to discover your roots and your passion for Scotland.

The biker-historian's unique combination of unabashed romanticism and easy irreverence make him the ideal guide to historical subjects all too easily swallowed up in maudlin sentiment or 'demythologised' by academic studies.
THE SCOTSMAN

Ross's patriotism is straightforward and unquestioning, albeit relieved by a pawky sense of humour.
THE HERALD

Blind Harry's Wallace

William Hamilton of Gilbertfield

Introduced by Elspeth King

Illustrations by Owain Kirby

ISBN 0 946487 33 2 PB £8.99

The original story of the real braveheart, Sir William Wallace. Racy, blood on every page, violently anglophobic, grossly embellished, vulgar and disgusting, clumsy and stilted, a literary failure, a great epic.

Whatever the verdict on BLIND HARRY, this is the book which has done more than any other to frame the notion of Scotland's national identity. Despite its numerous 'historical inaccuracies', it remains the principal source for what we now know about the life of Wallace.

The novel and film *Braveheart* were based on the 1722 Hamilton edition of this epic poem. Burns, Wordsworth, Byron and others were greatly influenced by this version 'wherein the old obsolete words are rendered more intelligible', which is said to be the book, next to the Bible, most commonly found in Scottish households in the eighteenth century. Burns even admits to having 'borrowed... a couplet worthy of Homer' directly from Hamilton's version of BLIND HARRY to include in 'Scots wha hae'.

Elspeth King, in her introduction to this, the first accessible edition of BLIND HARRY in verse form since 1859, draws parallels between the situation in Scotland at the time of Wallace and that in Bosnia and Chechnya in the 1990s. Seven hundred years to the day after the Battle of Stirling Bridge, the 'Settled Will of the Scottish People' was expressed in the devolution referendum of 11 September 1997. She describes this as a landmark opportunity for mature reflection on how the nation has been shaped, and sees BLIND HARRY'S WALLACE as an essential and compelling text for this purpose.

A true bard of the people.
TOM SCOTT, THE PENGUIN BOOK OF SCOTTISH VERSE, on Blind Harry.

A more inventive writer than Shakespeare.
RANDALL WALLACE

The story of Wallace poured a Scottish prejudice in my veins which will boil along until the floodgates of life shut in eternal rest.
ROBERT BURNS

Hamilton's couplets are not the best poetry you will ever read, but they rattle along at a fair pace. In re-issuing this work, the publishers have re-opened the spring from which most of our conceptions of the Wallace legend come.
SCOTLAND ON SUNDAY

The return of Blind Harry's Wallace, a man who makes Mel look like a wimp.
THE SCOTSMAN

Notes from the North incorporating a brief history of the Scots and the English

Emma Wood

ISBN 1 84282 048 6 PB £7.99

Notes on being English

Notes on being in Scotland

Learning from a shared past

Sickened by the English jingoism that surfaced in rampant form during the 1982 Falklands War, Emma Wood started to dream of moving from her home in East Anglia to the Highlands of Scotland.

She felt increasingly frustrated and marginalised as Thatcherism got a grip on the southern English psyche. The Scots she met on frequent holidays in the Highlands had no truck with Thatcherism, and she felt at home with grass-roots Scottish anti-authoritarianism. The decision was made. She uprooted and headed for a new life in the north of Scotland.

She was to discover that she had crossed a border in more than the geographical sense. In this book she sets a study of Scots-English conflicts alongside personal experiences of contemporary incomers' lives in the Highlands. Her own approach has been thoughtful and creative. *Notes from the North* is a pragmatic, positive and forward-looking contribution to cultural and political debate within Scotland.

... her enlightenment is evident on every page of this perceptive, provocative book.
MAIL ON SUNDAY

An intelligent and perceptive book... calm, reflective, witty and sensitive. It should certainly be read by all English visitors to Scotland, be they tourists or incomers. And it should certainly be read by all Scots concerned about what kind of nation we live in.
THE HERALD

Trident on Trial: the case for people's disarmament

Angie Zelter

ISBN 1 84282 004 4 PB £9.99

On a beautiful summer's evening in 1999, three women – Ellen Moxley, Ulla Roder and Angie Zelter – boarded a barge moored on a Scottish loch and threw some computer equipment overboard. Sheriff Margaret Gimblett acquitted 'The Trident Three' on the basis that they were acting as global citizens preventing nuclear crime. This led to what is thought to be the world's first High Court examination of the legality of an individual state's deployment of nuclear weapons...

Is Trident inherently unlawful and immoral?

When can a state use or threaten to use nuclear weapons?

Should international law take precedence over a sovereign government's?

Can a government be held accountable for ownership of weapons of mass destruction?

When is a citizen justified in acting against what she reasonably believes to be Government crime?

Is whose name does the UK government deploy 144 nuclear warheads, each around 10 times the power of that dropped on Hiroshima killing some 150,000 people?

This is Angie's personal account of the campaign. It also includes profiles of and contributions by some of the people and groups who have pledged to prevent nuclear crime in peaceful and practical ways. Without such public pressure governments will not abide by the Advisory Opinion nor implement their international agreements to abolish nuclear weapons.

This fine book should be read by everyone, especially those who have the slightest doubt that the world will one day be rid of nuclear weapons.
JOHN PILGER

Reading this book will help you play your part in keeping human life human.
REV DR ANDREW MacLELLAN, MODERATOR OF THE GENERAL ASSEMBLY OF THE CHURCH OF SCOTLAND 2000/2001

[Un]comfortably Numb: A Prison Requiem

Maureen Maguire

ISBN 1 84282 001 X PB £8.99

People may think I've taken the easy way out but please believe me this is the hardest thing I've ever had to do.

It was Christmas Eve, the atmosphere in Cornton Vale prison was festive, the girls in high spirits as they were locked up for the night. One of their favourite songs, Pink Floyd's *Comfortably Numb*, played loudly from a nearby cell as Yvonne Gilmour wrote her suicide note. She was the sixth of eight inmates to take their own lives in Cornton Vale prison over a short period of time.

[Un]comfortably Numb follows Yvonne through a difficult childhood, a chaotic adolescence and drug addiction to life and death behind bars. Her story is representative of many women in our prisons today. They are not criminals (only one per cent are convicted for violent crimes) and two-thirds are between the ages of 15 and 30. Suicide rates among them are rising dramatically. Do these vulnerable young girls really belong in prison?

This is a powerful and moving story told in the words of those involved: Yvonne and her family, fellow prisoners, prison officers, social workers, drug workers. It challenges us with questions which demand answers if more deaths are to be avoided.

Uncomfortably Numb is not a legal textbook or a jurisprudential treatise... it is an investigation into something our sophisticated society can't easily face. AUSTIN LAFFERTY

Reportage Scotland: History in the Making

Louise Yeoman
Foreword by Professor David Stevenson
ISBN 1 84282 051 6 PBK £6.99

 Events – both major and minor – as seen and recorded by Scots throughout history.

Which king was murdered in a sewer?

What was Dr Fian's love magic?

Who was the half-roasted abbot?
Which cardinal was salted and put in a barrel?
Why did Lord Kitchener's niece try to blow up Burns's cottage?

The answers can all be found in this eclectic mix covering nearly 2,000 years of Scottish history. Historian Louise Yeoman's rummage through the manuscript, book and newspaper archives of the National Library of Scotland has yielded an astonishing range of material from a letter to the king of the Picts to Mary Queen of Scots' own account of the murder of David Riccio; from the execution of William Wallace to accounts of anti-poll tax actions and the opening of the new Scottish Parliament. The book takes pieces from the original French, Latin, Gaelic and Scots and makes them accessible to the general reader, often for the first time.

The result is compelling reading for anyone interested in the history that has made Scotland what it is today.

... a marvellously illuminating and wonderfully readable book telling 'the story of Scotland' ... I find this almost intolerably moving. Yet many extracts made me laugh aloud.

Angus Calder, SCOTLAND ON SUNDAY

Absolutely inspired – a splendid selection of the quirky and the quintessential from Scotland's rumbustious history.

MAGNUS MAGNUSSON KBE

A monumental achievement in drawing together such a rich historical harvest.

Chris Holme, THE HERALD

NATURAL WORLD

The Hydro Boys: pioneers of renewable energy
Emma Wood
ISBN 1 84282 047 8 PB £8.99

Wild Scotland
James McCarthy
photographs by Laurie Campbell
ISBN 1 842820 96 6 PB £8.99

Wild Lives: Otters – On the Swirl of the Tide
Bridget MacCaskill
ISBN 0 946487 67 7 PB £9.99

Wild Lives: Foxes – The Blood is Wild
Bridget MacCaskill
ISBN 0 946487 71 5 PB £9.99

Scotland – Land & People: An Inhabited Solitude
James McCarthy
ISBN 0 946487 57 X PB £7.99

The Highland Geology Trail
John L Roberts
ISBN 0 946487 36 7 PB £5.99

Red Sky at Night
John Barrington
ISBN 0 946487 60 X PB £8.99

Listen to the Trees
Don MacCaskill
ISBN 0 946487 65 0 PB £9.99

THE QUEST FOR

The Quest for the Celtic Key
Karen Ralls-MacLeod and
Ian Robertson
ISBN 1 842820 84 2 PB £7.99

The Quest for Arthur
Stuart McHardy
ISBN 1 84282 012 5 HB £16.99

The Quest for the Nine Maidens
Stuart McHardy
ISBN 0 946487 66 9 HB £16.99

The Quest for Charles Rennie Mackintosh
John Cairney
ISBN 1 905222 43 2 PB £8.99

The Quest for Robert Louis Stevenson
John Cairney
ISBN 1 842820 85 0 PB £8.99

The Quest for the Original Horse Whisperers
Russell Lyon
ISBN 1 84282 020 6 HB £16.99

ON THE TRAIL OF

On the Trail of the Pilgrim Fathers
J. Keith Cheetham
ISBN 0 946487 83 9 PB £7.99

On the Trail of Mary Queen of Scots
J. Keith Cheetham
ISBN 0 946487 50 2 PB £7.99

On the Trail of John Wesley
J. Keith Cheetham
ISBN 1 84282 023 0 PB £7.99

On the Trail of William Wallace
David R. Ross
ISBN 0 946487 47 2 PB £7.99

On the Trail of Robert the Bruce
David R. Ross
ISBN 0 946487 52 9 PB £7.99

On the Trail of Robert Service
GW Lockhart
ISBN 0 946487 24 3 PB £7.99

On the Trail of John Muir
Cherry Good
ISBN 0 946487 62 6 PB £7.99

On the Trail of Robert Burns
John Cairney
ISBN 0 946487 51 0 PB £7.99

On t he Trail of Bonnie Prince Charlie
David R Ross
ISBN 0 946487 68 5 PB £7.99

On the Trail of Queen Victoria in the Highlands
Ian R Mitchell
ISBN 0 946487 79 0 PB £7.99

ISLANDS

The Islands that Roofed the World: Easdale, Belnahua, Luing & Seil:
Mary Withall
ISBN 0 946487 76 6 PB £4.99

Rum: Nature's Island
Magnus Magnusson
ISBN 0 946487 32 4 PB £7.95

LUATH GUIDES TO SCOTLAND

The North West Highlands: Roads to the Isles
Tom Atkinson
ISBN 1 842820 86 9 PB £6.99

Mull and Iona: Highways and Byways
Peter Macnab
ISBN 1 842820 89 3 PB £5.99

The Northern Highlands: The Empty Lands
Tom Atkinson
ISBN 1 842820 87 7 PB £6.99

The West Highlands: The Lonely Lands
Tom Atkinson
ISBN 1 842820 88 5 PB £6.99

South West Scotland
Tom Atkinson
ISBN 1 905222 15 7 PB £6.99

TRAVEL & LEISURE

Die Kleine Schottlandfibel [Scotland Guide in German]
Hans-Walter Arends
ISBN 1 842820 98 2 PB £8.99

Let's Explore Berwick-upon-Tweed
Anne Bruce English
ISBN 1 84282 029 X PB £4.99

Let's Explore Edinburgh Old Town
Anne Bruce English
ISBN 0 946487 98 7 PB £4.99

Edinburgh's Historic Mile
Duncan Priddle
ISBN 0 946487 97 9 PB £2.99

Pilgrims in the Rough: St Andrews beyond the 19th hole
Michael Tobert
ISBN 0 946487 74 X PB £7.99

FOOD & DRINK

The Whisky Muse: Scotch whisky in poem & song
various, compiled and edited by Robin Laing
ISBN 1 906307 44 X PB £9.99

First Foods Fast: how to prepare delicious simple meals for your baby, from first tastes to one year
Lara Boyd
ISBN 1 905222 46 7 PB £4.99

Edinburgh and Leith Pub Guide
Stuart McHardy
ISBN 0 946487 80 4 PB £4.95

WALK WITH LUATH

Hill Walks in the Cairngorms
Ernest Cross
ISBN 1 842820 92 3 PB £4.99

Easy Walks in Monarch of the Glen County: Badenoch and Strathspey
Ernest Cross
ISBN 1 842820 93 1 PB £4.99

The Joy of Hillwalking
Ralph Storer
ISBN 1 842820 69 9 PB £7.50

Scotland's Mountains before the Mountaineers
Ian R Mitchell
ISBN 0 946487 39 1 PB £9.99

Mountain Days & Bothy Nights
Dave Brown & Ian R Mitchell
ISBN 0 946487 15 4 PB £7.50

BIOGRAPHY

The Last Lighthouse
Sharma Krauskopf
ISBN 0 946487 96 0 PB £7.99

Tobermory Teuchter
Peter Macnab
ISBN 0 946487 41 3 PB £7.99

Bare Feet & Tackety Boots
Archie Cameron
ISBN 0 946487 17 0 PB £7.95

Come Dungeons Dark
John Taylor Caldwell
ISBN 0 946487 19 7 PB £6.95

SOCIAL HISTORY

Pumpherston: the story of a shale oil village
Sybil Cavanagh
ISBN 1 84282 015 X PB £10.99

Shale Voices
Alistair Findlay
ISBN 1 906307 11 3 PB £10.99

A Word for Scotland
Jack Campbell
ISBN 0 946487 48 0 PB £12.99

Crofting Years
Francis Thompson
ISBN 0 946487 06 5 PB £6.95

HISTORY

Desire Lines: A Scottish Odyssey
David R Ross
ISBN 1 84282 033 8 PB £9.99

Civil Warrior: extraordinary life & poems of Montrose
Robin Bell
ISBN 1 84282 013 3 HB £10.99

FOLKLORE

Luath Storyteller: Highland Myths & Legends
George W Macpherson
ISBN 1 84282 003 6 PB £5.00

Tales of the North Coast
Alan Temperley
ISBN 0 946487 18 9 PB £8.99

Tall Tales from an Island
Peter Macnab
ISBN 0 946487 07 3 PB £8.99

The Supernatural Highlands
Francis Thompson
ISBN 0 946487 31 6 PB £8.99

GENEALOGY

Scottish Roots: step-by-step guide for ancestor hunters
Alwyn James
ISBN 1 842820 90 7 PB £9.99

SPORT

Over the Top with the Tartan Army
Andy McArthur
ISBN 0 946487 45 6 PB £7.99

Ski & Snowboard Scotland
Hilary Parke
ISBN 0 946487 35 9 PB £6.99

FICTION

The Road Dance
John MacKay
ISBN 1 84282 040 0 PB £6.99

Milk Treading
Nick Smith
ISBN 1 84282 037 0 PB £6.99

The Strange Case of RL Stevenson
Richard Woodhead
ISBN 0 946487 86 3 HB £16.99

But n Ben A-Go-Go
Matthew Fitt
ISBN 1 905222 04 1 PB £7.99

Grave Robbers
Robin Mitchell
ISBN 0 946487 72 3 PB £7.99

The Bannockburn Years
William Scott
ISBN 0 946487 34 0 PB £7.95